# The New York Times

LOOKING FORWARD

# Trade Wars

## TARIFFS IN THE 21ST CENTURY

THE NEW YORK TIMES EDITORIAL STAFF

**Published in 2019 by New York Times Educational Publishing
in association with The Rosen Publishing Group, Inc.
29 East 21st Street, New York, NY 10010**

First Edition

**The New York Times**
Alex Ward: Editorial Director, Book Development
Phyllis Collazo: Photo Rights/Permissions Editor
Heidi Giovine: Administrative Manager

**Rosen Publishing**
Megan Kellerman: Managing Editor
Marcia Amidon Lusted: Editor
Greg Tucker: Creative Director
Brian Garvey: Art Director

**Cataloging-in-Publication Data**
Names: New York Times Company.
Title: Trade wars: tariffs in the 21st century / edited by the New
York Times editorial staff.
Description: New York : New York Times Educational Publishing,
2019. | Series: Looking forward | Includes glossary and index.
Identifiers: ISBN 9781642821406 (library bound) | ISBN
9781642821390 (pbk.) | ISBN 9781642821413 (ebook)
Subjects: LCSH: International trade—Juvenile literature. |
Foreign trade regulation—Juvenile literature.
Classification: LCC HF1379.T733 2019 | DDC 382'.92—dc23

*Manufactured in the United States of America*

**On the cover:** Shipping containers, many from China, are stacked
at the Port of Los Angeles in October 2013; Monica Almeida/The
New York Times.

# Contents

**CHAPTER 2**

# America First?

**CHAPTER 3**

# The World Responds

**CHAPTER 4**

# Escalation and Consequences

# Introduction

FOR AS LONG as the United States has been a country, and even when it was still a colony of Great Britain's, it has been engaged in trade with other countries. Trade allows countries to buy and sell goods and services from each other, providing economic benefits for each country and allowing citizens to buy what they need and what their own country may not be able to produce.

However, trade is not just about buying and selling. It also plays a big role in the relationships and alliances between countries. It can be used to establish friendly relationships between countries, or withdrawn to express displeasure over another country's policies and actions. An imbalance in trade, where one country imports more from other countries than it sells, can create a trade deficit. A trade surplus occurs when a country sells more goods than it imports.

Trade also brings with it the issue of tariffs, which are taxes imposed on goods as they pass from one country to another. Tariffs can be charged on imports and exports, and they are usually set as a way for a government to make money off trade with another country. However, they can also be used as a form of protectionism, which essentially makes goods from other countries more expensive so that consumers will buy goods made in their own countries, boosting those local manufacturers. Tariffs may also be placed on goods coming from another country as a punishment for that country's actions, such as military aggression or human rights violations. Governments can also create free trade agreements with each other, in which they have agreed not to charge each other tariffs on imported or exported goods.

From left: German Chancellor Angela Merkel, Canadian Prime Minister Justin Trudeau, President Donald Trump, French President Emmanuel Macron, European Commission President Jean-Claude Juncker and Japanese Prime Minister Shinzo Abe, at the G-7 summit meeting in La Malbaie, Quebec, Canada, June 8, 2018. Trump has found himself isolated on the global stage for taking actions viewed by America's closest allies as destructive and even illegal.

The United States has imposed tariffs throughout its history but has also participated in many free trade agreements and groups, such as the World Trade Organization (WTO), the North American Free Trade Agreement (Nafta), the South Korea and U.S. Free Trade Agreement and the Trans-Pacific Partnership (TPP).

When Donald J. Trump campaigned for president in 2016, one of his campaign promises revolved around helping American manufacturing jobs by renegotiating trade agreements and possibly placing tariffs on goods from other countries. Many Americans found his platform appealing because they felt that too many American factories and their jobs were being lost to foreign competition, particularly from places such as China, which could produce goods much more cheaply than the United States. Trump promised to impose tariffs on goods made in China and Mexico, whose products compete with those made in America, even though experts felt that imposing tariffs would violate international trade rules and also possibly spawn a trade war. He also said he was considering leaving the TPP and Nafta.

In early 2018, President Trump began levying tariffs on goods from countries such as China, Mexico and even Canada. The backlash from other countries has been strong, and even in the U.S. government, there are fears that these tariffs will actually hurt American businesses and consumers and may also start a trade war. To explore the issue of trade, tariffs and trade wars, it is necessary to look at some of the president's actions that have led to this point. It is also helpful to consider how his "Make America Great Again" slogan and economic protectionism have forced other countries to respond and how those responses may have affected the economies of both the United States and its partners, its relationship with its allies and the world economy. In an economy that is now global, with every country connected to others in a web of trade agreements and tariffs, what the United States does will undeniably have global repercussions.

# CHAPTER 1

# Tariffs and Trade

As President Trump began to address the issue of trade and tariffs and put into motion his campaign promises about protecting American jobs and companies, it created a storm of opinions about the possible and probable repercussions of enacting tariffs and withdrawing from established trade agreements. Economists warned of the effects on American industries, but President Trump continued with his plan to correct what he considered to be unfair practices against the United States by its trading partners.

## Will 2018 Be the Year of Protectionism? Trump Alone Will Decide

BY ANA SWANSON | JAN. 3, 2018

WASHINGTON — The Trump administration will soon face several major trade decisions that will determine whether the White House adopts the type of protectionist barriers that President Trump campaigned on but that were largely absent during his first year in office.

So far, the president's actions on trade have been more moderate than his campaign speeches suggested. Mr. Trump withdrew the United States from a Pacific Rim trade pact and opened other, existing trade deals to renegotiations. But he has yet to impose any of the broad tariffs that he has argued are necessary to give American companies a fair shot in a global economy.

In 2018, Mr. Trump will have several opportunities to punish foreign rivals as the final decider in a series of unusual trade cases that were initiated last year. These cases, which were brought under little-used provisions of trade laws, give the president broad authority to impose sweeping tariffs or quotas on foreign products.

The United States has numerous other routine trade cases in the works — like Boeing's fight with the Canadian plane maker Bombardier. But the ones heading to Mr. Trump's desk are unique because they fall to the president alone, rather than career bureaucrats, to decide.

"We're approaching a moment of truth where decisions have to be made to impose tariffs or not," said Wendy Cutler, vice president of the Asia Society Policy Institute and a former trade negotiator. "The days of saying we're going to have a study on this or carry out an investigation into that are over."

Many American companies, particularly manufacturers, are cheering on the administration. They argue that they need the government's assistance to stop foreign companies from flooding the market with cheap products.

But others, including consumers and companies that buy steel, aluminum, solar modules and other products, complain that tariffs would make these items more expensive, put American companies out of business and kill more jobs than they create. And some of the measures the Trump administration is considering might violate commitments that the United States has made under existing trade pacts, risking retaliation from other countries.

## CHINESE IMPORTS AND INVESTMENT

The president has long hammered China for taking advantage of the United States on trade, and threatened to impose penalties as a result. Now, with a special investigation on China drawing to a close, he appears to have his chance.

In August, the administration opened an investigation into whether China's actions on intellectual property were harming the United

States. The investigation has focused on technology transfer, in which China forces or coerces companies to share intellectual property as a condition of doing business there. It's a practice that could help Chinese producers gain an advantage over American competitors in years to come.

The results of the investigation aren't due until August, but trade analysts say they could arrive within weeks. They suggest that the administration might consider restrictions on Chinese investment in the United States, as well as tariffs on Chinese products.

In an interview with The New York Times on Dec. 28, the president said that he had been "soft on China" to gain the country's help on North Korea, but that he was now intent on cracking down.

"China on trade has ripped off this country more than any other element of the world in history has ripped off anything," he said. "If they don't help us with North Korea, then I do what I've always said I want to do."

The United States typically takes cases against foreign competitors after investigations like these to the World Trade Organization. But the Trump administration has suggested that it may not want to wait for the World Trade Organization. If the United States acts alone, it may violate the organization's rules. In that case, China could gain the support of other World Trade Organization members and retaliate against the United States with its own trade restrictions, potentially triggering a trade war between the world's two largest economies.

## SOLAR PRODUCTS

The president must decide by Jan. 26 whether to impose tariffs or quotas on imports of solar cells and modules. Imposing restrictions could make solar products more expensive, slowing the adoption of solar power. But the domestic manufacturers argue that without protection from cheap Chinese products, American solar manufacturing will disappear.

Two companies, Suniva and SolarWorld, have asked for broader protections by bringing a so-called "safeguard case" — a rarely used measure that gives the president broad power to help a struggling industry. This type of power has not been used to levy tariffs since 2002, when President George W. Bush restricted imports of steel.

On Oct. 31, a panel of trade officials who had studied the case recommended that the president impose restrictions, with some arguing for tariffs of up to 35 percent on some products. The final decision rests with the president.

## WASHING MACHINES

A similar safeguard case, related to imported washing machines, is now headed to Mr. Trump for a final decision.

Whirlpool has petitioned the government to restrict low-cost imports, which it says have flooded the market and hurt American manufacturers. It claims that South Korean rivals Samsung and LG have moved their production around the globe to evade American tariffs that were levied on specific countries. As a result, it has asked for broader protections that a safeguard case can bring.

Trade officials reviewing the case recommended that the United States impose some restrictions on imports, by taxing them after a certain number of washers enter the American market each year.

But Whirlpool and its supporters — including Ohio's senators, Rob Portman, a Republican, and Sherrod Brown, a Democrat — have urged the president to adopt even tougher restrictions to preserve American manufacturing. Mr.Trump must make the final decision by Feb. 2.

## STEEL AND ALUMINUM

The most contentious trade cases the president will have to weigh in on are twin investigations regarding imports of steel and aluminum.

The Trump administration opened an investigation on April 19 into how much steel the United States needs to protect its national security, and whether current capacity meets that level. Carried out under Section 232 of the 1962 Trade Expansion Act, the case would allow the president to impose sweeping barriers on steel imports.

The plan garnered swift support from steelworkers, steel companies and Rust Belt legislators. They say the industry is struggling to remain in the United States, putting the ability to manufacture weapons, tanks and critical infrastructure in jeopardy.

Users of steel, including carmakers, food companies and the military, have expressed concern about the potential for higher costs.

Some American allies, like Germany, South Korea, Canada and Japan, have also protested, saying the burden of tariffs could fall heavily on their companies. Steel makers mostly point to a flood of cheap Chinese steel, but the United States already heavily restricts imports from China. Supporters of tariffs say Chinese steel is flooding into the United States through other countries, and the United States would look to impose a broad solution to cut off the foreign flow of Chinese steel.

The Commerce Department must submit its report on the investigation by Jan. 15 to the president, who will have 90 days to determine an action.

A similar investigation into aluminum imports was started on April 26, and the Commerce Department must submit its findings to the president by Jan. 21. Mr. Trump will then have 90 days to make a decision.

If the United States does restrict steel and aluminum imports, other countries might go after the United States at the World Trade Organization. The question then would be whether the Trump administration would choose to heed the World Trade Organization's directives or ignore them, potentially undermining the global group.

# G.M. Chief Cautions Trump Administration on Upending Nafta

BY NEAL E. BOUDETTE | JAN. 16, 2018

DETROIT — General Motors' chief executive urged the Trump administration on Tuesday not to scrap the North American Free Trade Agreement, and said any changes in the pact should account for the effect on American automakers and workers.

"There could be unintended consequences, changes made, that would directly impact jobs in the United States," the G.M. chief, Mary T. Barra, said at an investor conference on the sidelines of the Detroit auto show. "Nafta needs to be modified," she added, but she rejected the idea that "we need to walk away from it."

As part of a push to create American jobs, President Trump has said that Nafta should be renegotiated and has at times suggested that the United States could withdraw from the agreement or tax vehicles imported from Mexico, where G.M. makes certain small cars, sport-utility vehicles and pickup trucks.

Saying she favored steps to modernize the agreement, Ms. Barra added, "We are completely aligned with the administration on job preservation." She said G.M. had had discussions with officials from the United States, Mexico and Canada "to make sure everybody understands the complexity" of how the pact affects automakers and the flow of parts and vehicles across borders within North America.

Fiat Chrysler Automobiles announced last week that it was moving production of its heavy-duty pickup trucks from Mexico to Michigan. On Monday, Sergio Marchionne, the company's chief executive, said that the move eased any concerns that the company could be hurt by a border tax or other possible changes to Nafta.

Negotiations over the future of Nafta have been tense. The next round is to begin next Tuesday in Montreal.

Mark Reuss, General Motors' executive vice president for global product development, introducing a line of 2019 Chevrolet Silverados on the eve of the Detroit auto show.

At the investor conference, sponsored by Deutsche Bank, G.M. said it expected 2017 earnings to come in at the high end of its forecast of $6 to $6.50 a share, and it projected its 2018 earnings at roughly the same level. The company, which earned $6.12 per share in 2016, predicted "further acceleration" in 2019.

Still, the company's chief financial officer, Chuck Stevens, acknowledged "headwinds" in the form of pricing pressure in the American and Chinese markets and high costs related to the introduction of a new generation of full-size pickups. Over all, new-vehicle sales in the United States are also expected to decline modestly this year.

Mr. Stevens also said that G.M. would take a $7 billion noncash charge against earnings in the fourth quarter of 2017. That reflects the decline in value of certain tax credits the company has on its balance sheet — a result of the recently enacted tax law, which lowered corporate rates.

G.M. is also losing money or making very little on the cars it sells. With American consumers flocking to roomier models like trucks and S.U.V.s, sales of cars like the Chevrolet Malibu and Impala have plunged. G.M. slashed production at many of its car plants last year.

While struggling to keep its car lines profitable, G.M. is generating a substantial profit on truck sales and making more S.U.V.s and trucks to take advantage of the trend. The 2019 Chevy Silverado, showcased this week at the Detroit show, will be available in eight variations, said Dan Ammann, the automaker's president. G.M. also plans to introduce new medium-duty pickup trucks, a lucrative business it exited several years ago.

"We see a ton more opportunity" in trucks, Mr. Ammann said.

Ford and Fiat Chrysler are following the same strategy. Ford has unveiled a new midsize truck, resurrecting the Ranger name, at the Detroit show. Fiat Chrysler is adding a new Ram 1500 truck and expanding its line of Jeeps.

At the same conference, Ford Motor offered a less upbeat outlook. The company said preliminary results showed it earned $1.95 per share in 2017, up from $1.15 the year before. But for 2018, company officials said its adjusted earnings would fall to $1.45 to $1.70 per share, compared with an adjusted 2017 figure of $1.78.

Ford's chief financial officer, Robert L. Shanks, blamed rising commodity prices and unfavorable exchange rates as well as higher spending on self-driving vehicles and lower industry sales in the United States. "We are not satisfied with our performance," he said.

Ford said it was not taking any charges stemming from the tax legislation.

Ford has kicked off a cost-cutting drive under Jim Hackett, who was tapped last year to be chief executive to reinvigorate the company. As part of its new direction, Ford is spending billions in an effort to introduce 40 electrified vehicles by 2022, including 16 fully electric models. It also hopes to begin producing a driverless car for taxi fleets, rider services and delivery companies by 2021.

# Trump's Solar Tariffs Are Clouding the Industry's Future

BY ANA SWANSON AND BRAD PLUMER | JAN. 23, 2018

ZEBULON, N.C. — At this century-old farm just outside Durham, symmetrical rows of shining blue solar panels have replaced the soybeans and tobacco that Tommy Vinson and his family used to grow here. It is one of many solar farms that have sprung up around North Carolina, transforming a state long battered by global offshoring into the second-largest generator of solar electricity after California.

"It's still reaping a very good harvest," said April Vinson, who is married to Tommy. "It's just not a traditional kind of farm."

Across North Carolina, textile factories and tobacco farms have disappeared, giving way to fields of solar panels.

The ABD solar farm in Asheboro, N.C., above. North Carolina is the second-largest generator of solar electricity after California.

But for those venturing into solar farming like Mr. Vinson, the future of this vibrant industry is now cloudy. On Monday, the Trump administration announced that it would impose steep tariffs on imported solar panels, which could raise the cost of solar power in the years ahead, slowing adoption of the technology and costing jobs.

Mr. Trump has long championed trade barriers as a way to protect United States manufacturers from foreign competitors. On Monday, he also slapped tariffs on imported washing machines, and his advisers say additional measures on steel, aluminum and other products will soon be coming.

"Our action today helps to create jobs in America for Americans," Mr. Trump said on Tuesday in the Oval Office.

The two solar companies that had sought the tariffs, Suniva and SolarWorld Americas, argue that low-cost imports have decimated American manufacturing of solar cells and modules in recent years.

Today, 95 percent of the solar panels used in the United States are imported from countries like Malaysia and South Korea, and the companies contend that tariffs are needed to protect the nation's remaining solar factories.

"Today the president is sending a message that American innovation and manufacturing will not be bullied out of existence without a fight," Suniva said on Monday.

But while the tariffs may help domestic manufacturers, they are expected to ripple throughout the industry in ways that may ultimately hurt American companies and their workers. Energy experts say it is unlikely that the tariffs will create more than a small number of American solar manufacturing jobs, since low-wage countries will continue to have a competitive edge.

Solar manufacturing now represents just a fraction of the overall jobs that have developed around the solar industry. More than 260,000 Americans are employed in the sector, but fewer than 2,000 of those employed in the United States are manufacturing solar cells and modules, according to the Solar Energy Industries Association.

An electrician at the ABD solar farm in Asheboro. The tariffs may help domestic manufacturers, but they are expected to affect the industry in ways that may ultimately hurt American companies and their workers.

Far more workers are employed in areas that underpin the use of solar technology, such as making steel racks that angle the panels toward the sun. And the bulk of workers in the solar industry install and maintain the projects, a process that is labor-intensive and hard to automate.

The tariffs the president announced start at 30 percent next year and ultimately fall to 15 percent by the fourth year. In each of the four years, the first 2.5 gigawatts of imported solar cells will be exempted from the tariff.

But by raising the cost of one all-important ingredient, the tariffs could make solar power less competitive with other sources of energy, like gas and wind, resulting in the construction of fewer solar projects. On Tuesday, the Solar Energy Industries Association said that the president's action would result in the loss of roughly 23,000 jobs in the solar industry this year, as well as the delay or cancellation of billions of dollars of investments.

At the Wakefield solar farm, the five-megawatt project on the Vinson family's land, the cells that collect solar energy are imported — they were manufactured by JA Solar, a Chinese company, which makes cells and panels in China and Malaysia.

But the steel frames that the panels rest on are American made, manufactured by RBI Solar, which is based in Cincinnati. The steel that RBI Solar used to make these racks is also American, bought from Worthington Industries in Ohio and Attala Steel in Mississippi.

The project was developed and is now operated by Cypress Creek Renewables, a growing company that employs engineers, electricians and drone pilots in a new glass and brick office building in Durham. It was built by Horne Brothers Construction, which at the project's peak hired about 50 people to drive piles and install the solar panels.

And then there are the Vinsons, the farming family who now have a steady income from leasing their land that allowed Tommy's mother, Martha, to comfortably retire.

On a brisk day this month, the Vinsons sidestepped puddles of melting snow as they walked through rows of solar panels. But the sun was still shining, and the air above the panels shimmered with heat. Built on a 30-acre site, the project now produces enough power for 1,000 homes — including, potentially, that of the Vinsons, who live just a mile away.

In North Carolina, state laws and tax incentives that favor solar projects selling power directly to the electrical grid have helped the industry expand to the point where it now powers more than 400,000 homes and employs around 7,000 people.

"Everything you see here, with the exception of the module, was built in America," said Tom Kosto, the executive vice president of Horne Brothers Construction.

Mr. Kosto's company has expanded in the last three years to 350 full-time employees, from just 30, and he said he planned to hire 100 more people this year. He pays his employees an average of $17.31, with benefits. But he said the tariffs would force his company to cut back on its expansion plans.

"We're a profitable company, but with one stroke of the pen, they can take that away," Mr. Kosto said. "All you're doing is you're putting thousands of jobs at risk for jobs that aren't coming back."

The move is expected to hit utility-scale solar projects like this one, which sell their electricity to power companies, particularly hard. Home and business owners may decide to continue buying solar panels for their rooftops, even if the price is a little higher. But when solar projects sell to a utility company, they compete with other sources of energy, and every cent counts.

Over the last eight years, an influx of cheap imported panels has driven down the cost of solar projects by 85 percent, according to Lazard, a financial advisory company. As a result, the number of solar installations has soared to 12 gigawatts last year, from less than one gigawatt in 2010.

While the tariffs are likely to slow the adoption of solar power in the United States, they will not entirely halt the industry. An analysis by GTM Research found that solar installations will continue to rise from 2018 to 2022, though there will be 11 percent fewer panels installed as a result of the tariffs.

One reason for the muted effect: Solar cells and modules account for one-third or less of the overall cost of solar systems, and the industry has been relentlessly cutting the costs of all components. All told, the tariffs will increase the cost of utility-scale solar projects by about 10 percent and residential rooftop systems by just 3 percent — raising them roughly to prices seen two years ago.

But even a small price increase could slow the industry's growth in states where solar already faces fierce competition from cheap natural gas, such as Florida, Georgia, South Carolina or Texas. "In the Southeast in particular, we were just starting to see solar compete at the margins with natural gas," said MJ Shiao, a solar analyst at GTM Research.

Duke Energy, a major utility company in North Carolina, said Tuesday that the tariff would cause it to carefully evaluate the economics of each of its solar projects. The company currently owns more than 800 megawatts of solar power capacity and had planned to build and buy more than 3,000 megawatts in the next five years.

Many analysts say the tariff may fall short of its goal of reviving solar manufacturing in the United States. While at least one company has reportedly expressed interest in opening a 1,000-worker module assembly plant in Jacksonville, Fla., that is likely to be a rare case.

"This tariff only puts module prices back to where they were in 2015 or 2016, and U.S. manufacturers weren't competitive then," said Varun Sivaram, an expert on solar power at the Council on Foreign Relations.

In the meantime, the companies involved with the long rows of solar panels that have cropped up on the Vinson's land — Cypress Creek, the project's designer; RBI Solar, which made the mounting system; and Horne Brothers Construction — expect to be hurt by the measure.

"Every percentage point of tariff is going to mean projects which will no longer be built, because they are no longer economically viable," said Matthew McGovern, the chief executive of Cypress Creek Renewables. "We'll lose projects, no question."

# Trump Authorizes Tariffs, Defying Allies at Home and Abroad

BY PETER BAKER AND ANA SWANSON | MARCH 8, 2018

WASHINGTON — President Trump defied opposition from his own party and protests from overseas as he signed orders on Thursday imposing stiff and sweeping new tariffs on imported steel and aluminum. But he sought to soften the impact on the United States' closest allies with a more flexible plan than originally envisioned.

After a week of furious lobbying and a burst of last-minute internal debates and confusion, Mr. Trump agreed to exempt, for now, Canada and Mexico, and held out the possibility of later excluding allies like Australia. But foreign leaders warned of a trade war that could escalate to other industries and take aim at American goods.

"The actions we are taking today are not a matter of choice; they are a matter of necessity for our security," Mr. Trump said in a ceremony at the White House where he officially authorized the tariffs, which will go into effect in 15 days.

Flanked by a handful of steel and aluminum workers, some wearing coveralls and holding hard hats, Mr. Trump presented the move as a way to rebuild vital industries decimated by foreign competition. "Our factories were left to rot and to rust all over the place; thriving communities turned into ghost towns," he said. "That betrayal is now over."

The orders were Mr. Trump's most expansive use of federal power to rewrite the rules of global trade since he took office and upended the prevailing consensus on free markets that has largely governed Washington under administrations of both parties for decades. A longtime critic of globalization, Mr. Trump argued that the United States had been ravaged by unfair trading partners.

As a result of Mr. Trump's action, levies on imports of steel will rise by 25 percent and aluminum by 10 percent. Business groups have warned that the effect could be felt across the global supply network

President Trump signed an order imposing stiff and sweeping new tariffs on imported steel and aluminum at the White House on Thursday.

as consumers face higher prices for automobiles, appliances and other goods. But Mr. Trump's aides dismissed such predictions as "fake news" and said most Americans would hardly notice any impact.

The United States issued the tariffs under a little-used provision of trade law, which allows the president to take broad action to defend American national security. The Commerce Department previously determined that imports of metals posed a threat to national security.

The United States is the largest steel importer in the world and the order could hit South Korea, China, Japan, Germany, Turkey and Brazil the hardest. Mr. Trump said his tariff orders were tailored to give him the authority to raise or lower levies on a country-by-country basis and add or take countries off the list as he deemed appropriate.

"This has certainly put the fear of God in America's trading partners," said Eswar Prasad, a professor of international trade at Cornell University. The tariffs disprove the notion that Congress and broader business interests would prevent the Trump administration from turning its saber-rattling into real sanctions, Mr. Prasad said. "The day has actually come when real trade sanctions are on the board."

The White House sought to soften the blow by temporarily exempting two key trading partners, Canada and Mexico, and opening the door to carve-outs for other countries. Mr. Trump said the order would temporarily exempt Canada and Mexico, pending discussions with both about the terms of trade, including already tense talks over the North American Free Trade Agreement.

Officials from Canada and Mexico have said they will not be bullied into accepting a Nafta deal that could disadvantage their countries.

Chrystia Freeland, Canada's foreign minister, called the initial exemption a "step forward" but said it would not change Canada's negotiating approach to Nafta. In a statement, Mexico said those talks would not be subject to conditions outside the negotiating process.

In language authorizing the tariffs, the White House said any nation with a security relationship with the United States was welcome to discuss "alternative ways to address the threatened impairment of the national security caused by imports from that country." Those talks could result in the tariff being lifted, the order said.

Mr. Trump said that Robert Lighthizer, the top United States trade negotiator, would be in charge of negotiating with countries asking for exemptions in the next 15 days.

The potential for exemptions is likely to incite a tsunami of lobbying and cajoling as foreign governments pressure the White House for a carve-out that could save them from steep tariffs.

"We look forward to educating the Trump administration on the vital role the Japanese steel industry plays in the American marketplace," said Tadaaki Yamaguchi, a steel executive and the chairman of the Japan Steel Information Center. "The Japanese industry is not part of the import problem but a solution."

Wilbur Ross, the commerce secretary, will lead a parallel process that could result in the exemption of certain products made of steel and aluminum that American companies need, but that are not manufactured domestically. Products as varied as construction cranes and railroad ties are made with specialized steel that is not available widely, if at all, from United States manufacturers.

During a cabinet meeting earlier in the day, Mr. Trump singled out Australia as an example of another country that could be excluded, citing the trade surplus that the United States maintains with Australia, which imports more from America than it exports to the country.

The announced trade barriers came just hours after a group of countries signed the Trans-Pacific Partnership, a sweeping trade deal that no longer includes the United States. Mr. Trump, a fervent opponent of the deal, officially withdrew the United States from it on his fourth day in office.

The juxtaposition further highlighted the protectionist approach to trade policy that Mr. Trump has embraced, bucking years of America's embrace of free and open trade. Trade experts said the approach would ultimately compromise the United States' ability to temper China's unfair trading practices.

"The tariff action coupled with the mishandled renegotiations of existing trade deals have alienated the very countries we need as allies to help confront the challenges posed by China," said Daniel M. Price, a former Bush White House adviser.

The tariff announcement was poised to set off a wave of retaliation and suits against the United States at the World Trade Organization, as countries argue that they posed no security threat to the United States.

Trade lawyers said that, by exempting Canada and Mexico from the process for reasons related to Nafta, the United States might undermine its legal argument for national security and open itself up to further challenges.

They also worried about the ultimate consequences of those trade cases for an international trading system that the United States has worked to construct since World War II.

If the World Trade Organization rules against the United States, the Trump administration will have to decide whether to reverse its decision or go up against the organization. If the United States ignores or withdraws from the group, it could precipitate a breakdown in global trading rules and a new era of global protectionism.

"It opens up this horrible Pandora's box, and we don't know where that leaves other countries or where that leaves the W.T.O.," said Monica de Bolle, a senior fellow at the Peterson Institute for International Economics.

Mario Draghi, the president of the European Central Bank, said on Thursday that a plan to impose broad tariffs that hit allies was "dangerous" and could undermine national security.

"If you put tariffs against your allies," Mr. Draghi said at a news conference in Frankfurt, "one wonders who the enemies are."

More than 100 Republican lawmakers sent a letter to Mr. Trump on Wednesday imploring him to drop plans for sweeping tariffs. A day earlier, Mr. Trump's chief economic adviser, Gary D. Cohn, announced his resignation after his failure to forestall the president from pursuing tariffs.

While many economists have said it is natural for a high-technology, highly developed economy like the United States to evolve away from raw industries, Mr. Trump presented the steel and aluminum sectors in romantic terms, signs of a muscular superpower that had been allowed to atrophy under his predecessors.

"Steel is steel," he said. "You don't have steel, you don't have a country."

He invited a few of the steelworkers to make comments and they told stories of plants that have cut back or idled altogether. "These tariffs going into place, this gives us the ability to come back to 100 percent capacity," said Dustin Stevens, a worker at Century Aluminum's plant in Hawesville, Ky.

Century Aluminum has said that it will restart shuttered capacity at its Hawesville plant, adding nearly 300 workers this year. And on

Wednesday, United States Steel said it would restart a blast furnace in Granite City, Ill., bringing back 500 workers to help meet additional orders that it expected as a result of the tariffs.

But economists warned of potential job losses from price increases, and other industries that send their products abroad denounced the risk of retaliation. John Heisdorffer, the president of the American Soybean Association, called the tariffs "a disastrous course of action from the White House" that could put farmers at risk at a time when the agriculture industry is already struggling. "We have heard directly from the Chinese that U.S. soybeans are prime targets for retaliation," he said. Soybeans are the United States' biggest agricultural export.

Senator Ben Sasse, Republican of Nebraska, said the United States was "on the verge of a painful and stupid trade war."

"This isn't just bad for farmers and ranchers in Nebraska who need to buy a new tractor, it's also bad for the moms and dads who will lose their manufacturing jobs because fewer people can buy a more expensive product," he said.

Senator Mitch McConnell of Kentucky, the majority leader, said he and his colleagues "are concerned about the scope of the proposed tariffs on steel and aluminum and their impact on American citizens and businesses, including many I represent in Kentucky."

In 2002, President George W. Bush imposed steel tariffs of up to 30 percent. But facing an adverse ruling by the World Trade Organization and retaliation by trading partners, he lifted them 15 months before the end of the planned three-year duration. Studies found that more jobs were lost than saved and Republican leaders vowed not to repeat the experiment.

The Trade Partnership, a research firm cited by pro-trade advocates, has concluded the same would happen with Mr. Trump's tariffs. It estimated that the tariffs would create 33,464 jobs in the metals sectors but cost 179,334 jobs in other sectors for a net loss of nearly 146,000.

The issue has divided Mr. Trump's own team. Mr. Ross, Mr. Lighthizer and Peter Navarro, the president's trade and manufacturing adviser, overcame objections from Mr. Cohn and national security officials like Jim Mattis, the defense secretary, who cautioned Mr. Trump that the plan would roil relations with important security allies.

The consequences of the split were on display at the cabinet meeting earlier in the day when Mr. Trump thanked Mr. Cohn for his service, but needled him about his decision to leave. "He may be a globalist, but I still like him," the president said as Mr. Cohn sat in a chair along the wall and smiled. "He's seriously a globalist. There's no question. You know what? In his own way he's a nationalist, because he loves his country."

Mr. Trump then suggested that Mr. Cohn might eventually return to the administration. "I have a feeling you'll be back," the president said. In a teasing voice, he added: "I don't know if I can put him in the same position though. He's not quite as strong on those tariffs as we want."

# U.S. Exempts Some Allies From Tariffs, but May Opt for Quotas

BY JIM TANKERSLEY AND NATALIE KITROEFF | MARCH 22, 2018

WASHINGTON — The Trump administration began imposing stiff tariffs on imported steel and aluminum early on Friday morning. But it granted a brief exemption to some allies, and in a twist, said it might impose import quotas to prevent too much foreign metal from flooding into the United States.

The White House detailed the decision in a pair of presidential proclamations late Thursday night. They gave allies that won exemptions a May 1 deadline to negotiate "satisfactory alternative means" to address what the administration calls the threat to United States national security resulting from its current levels of steel and aluminum imports. The exempted group includes Canada, Mexico, the European Union, Australia, Argentina, Brazil and South Korea.

President Trump also said in the proclamation that he would "consider" directing Customs and Border Protection to put in place a quota on imports from the exempted countries before the May 1 deadline, "if necessary and appropriate." Mr. Trump wrote that he would "take into account all steel articles imports since Jan. 1, 2018, in setting the amount of such quota."

The announcement also left the door open for other allies that did not win exemptions, most notably Japan, to negotiate with the administration over tariffs. "Any country not listed in this proclamation with which we have a security relationship remains welcome to discuss with the United States alternative ways to address the threatened impairment of the national security caused by imports of steel articles from that country," Mr. Trump wrote.

The shift in strategy reflects a few chaotic weeks in which foreign governments lobbied, cajoled and threatened Washington to win exemptions from the 25 percent tariffs on steel and the 10 percent tariffs on aluminum.

Peter Navarro, a top trade adviser to Mr. Trump, said Thursday in a television appearance that the White House would impose quotas.

"Every country that is not facing tariffs that we're going to negotiate with will face quotas so that we protect our aluminum and steel industries," Mr. Navarro said on CNN. "For all countries, there has to be a quota. If you don't put a quota on, then any country that can do whatever they want will become a transshipment point for every other country."

The proclamation issued late Thursday declares that Mr. Trump will consult with the director of the National Economic Council, along with United States trade representative Robert Lighthizer and others, in determining any possible quotas.

It also said Mr. Trump would decide by May 1 whether to continue to exempt those countries, based on the status of negotiations, and it held open the possibility that he could modify the tariffs affecting other countries at any time.

Many of the countries that were exempted are engaged in trade talks in which the United States is trying to win concessions. That includes Canada and Mexico, which are in the midst of renegotiating the North American Free Trade Agreement, and South Korea, which is renegotiating its free-trade pact with the United States.

Japan has been a source of ire for Mr. Trump, who has criticized its trade practices going back to the 1980s. The two nations made only modest progress in their economic dialogue last year, with the United States pushing for a new bilateral trade agreement that would ease restrictions on American exports of beef and cars to Japan.

The tariff exemptions could help prevent retaliatory trade barriers that other trading partners had threatened, including the European Union, which said it would target American exports like Florida orange juice, peanut butter and motorcycles.

It would also provide some relief to American companies that use foreign metals in the products they use and make, like oil and gas pipelines, beer cans and food packaging.

But the move caught those who support the tariffs, including the American steel industry, by surprise.

"Everyone is kind of freaking out," said Philip K. Bell, president of the Steel Manufacturers Association. He said he was waiting to see the final details of the policy but would have wanted the exclusions to be much more narrow. "This represents a lot of tons of imports that find their way to our shores, and this could have the effect of watering down" Mr. Trump's trade action.

Imposing quotas would offer some help, Mr. Bell said, because without the limits, American companies would face incentives to start buying their steel from excluded countries and domestic mills would be right back where they were pre-tariffs. The exempted countries account for more than half of the $29 billion in steel sold to the United States in 2017.

Quotas are viewed as less aggressive than tariffs because foreign exporters tend to benefit from the constraints, in the form of higher prices, while in the case of tariffs, the United States government picks up the higher duties.

"It may be more palatable for countries to accept quotas in the form of voluntary export restraints than accept an increase in tariffs," said Monica de Bolle, a senior fellow at the Peterson Institute for International Economics. "Tariffs are seen as very unfriendly by other countries because it's a unilateral action rather than a negotiated action."

Mr. Lighthizer outlined the exemptions during questioning Thursday morning in the Senate Finance Committee.

"The idea that the president has is that, based on a certain set of criteria, some countries should be out," Mr. Lighthizer said. "What he has decided to do is pause the implementation of the tariffs in respect to those countries."

The White House imposed the tariffs by citing a section of trade law that gives the president authority to limit imports to protect national security. The Commerce Department said the metals were a national security risk because they were degrading the American industrial base.

The administration then floated the potential for exemptions, intimating that nations could be excluded if they found other ways to resolve the national security concerns and to reduce their trade deficit with the United States.

The United States runs a trade deficit with many nations, including China and Japan, importing more goods from those countries than it exports. Last year, Japan sent about $1.7 billion in steel mill products to the United States, according to IHS Markit Global Trade Atlas. Without an exclusion, it will be the only one of the top six foreign suppliers of steel to the United States to face steep tariffs.

Japanese steel makers argue that they hardly compete with American steel mills, because they make niche, specialized products that are not replicated here, rather than undercutting prices by flooding the market with a cheap commodity.

Tadaaki Yamaguchi, chairman of the Japan Steel Information Center, a New York-based trade group, said failing to give Japan the same exemption that was extended to South Korea and Brazil was "an outrage and a travesty."

If the exempted countries are not subject to any export limits, the administration may need to raise tariffs on all the others if it wants to keep its promise to protect American producers on price. That would hit Japan harder than anyone.

The leaders of several countries with close ties, including military alliances, with the United States had warned that the restrictions could touch off a trade war and undercut a global economic recovery. They also argued that the tariffs would be mutually destructive and ignore the complexity of modern supply networks.

For example, the German carmaker BMW operates its largest factory in Spartanburg, S.C., buying about two-thirds of the steel it needs in the United States and importing the rest. BMW is also the largest exporter of cars made in the United States, with China being one of the main buyers, said Harald Krüger, the company's chief executive. "None of this would be possible without free trade," Mr. Krüger said in Munich on Wednesday.

# The Trade Issue That Most Divides U.S. and China Isn't Tariffs

BY KEITH BRADSHER AND ALAN RAPPEPORT | MARCH 26, 2018

BEIJING — China has struck a hard stance on the issue at the root of the looming trade fight between Beijing and Washington: China's government-led drive, which Washington describes as breaking international rules, to build the cutting-edge industries of the future.

Chinese officials in recent days have been defending the government's ambitious plan, known as Made in China 2025, to create globally competitive players in industries like advanced microchips, driverless cars and robotics. While Beijing has signaled a willingness to compromise on other matters, the intractable standoff over its core industrial policy could prolong a trade fight that has already shaken markets and led to concerns about a full-blown trade war.

"We are three years into the implementation of Made in China 2025, and we will keep going," Miao Wei, China's minister of industry and information technology, said on Monday, the last day of a three-day economic policy forum in the Chinese capital.

The Trump administration has threatened to impose tariffs on imports involving many of the industries being developed under the Made in China 2025 program. Administration officials strongly object to the program's goal of having Chinese companies dominate these advanced industries, particularly in the Chinese market.

Washington has also protested that companies in the targeted industries have been offered loans at low interest rates by state-controlled Chinese banks. The White House argues that will result in global capacity gluts that could drive down prices and destroy the viability of tech companies in the West, as well as in countries, like Japan and South Korea, that are allied with the United States.

"China has engaged for a very long time in the theft of our intellectual property as well as practices like forced technology transfer,"

Peter Navarro, President Trump's trade adviser, said on CNBC on Monday. "We're hopeful that China will basically work with us to address some of these practices."

Mr. Navarro on Monday tried to calm financial markets, which were rattled last week by the prospect of a trade war. He emphasized that "growth and stability" were the aim of Mr. Trump's policy goal of ensuring that trade with the United States is fair and reciprocal.

Investors' fears of a trade war seemed to subside some on Monday. The Standard & Poor's 500-stock index climbed 2.7 percent, the Dow Jones industrial average rose 2.8 percent and the Nasdaq composite jumped 3.3 percent.

Whether an agreement that forestalls a protracted economic conflict can be reached remains unclear. The two nations, whose markets are highly integrated, have engaged in discussions for years with little to show as a result. Talks between the United States and China stalled last summer, and the Comprehensive Economic Dialogue between two countries has produced little progress.

The Trump administration has largely shunned the highly structured discussions of past administrations, which were used to try to reach agreement on economic and security issues. The White House now views those channels as producing largely hollow promises by the Chinese and has shifted toward engaging directly with senior-level Chinese counterparts.

On Saturday, just two days after the administration announced tariffs on up to $60 billion worth of Chinese imports, Steven Mnuchin, the Treasury secretary, called Liu He, China's economic czar, to congratulate him on his new role of vice premier. The two discussed the trade tensions, including reducing tariffs on American cars and opening up China's financial services sector to American firms.

"They also discussed the trade deficit between our two countries and committed to continuing the dialogue to find a mutually agreeable way to reduce it," a Treasury spokeswoman said.

China's official news agency, Xinhua, characterized the call between Mr. Mnuchin and Mr. Liu as confrontational, with Mr. Liu warning Mr. Mnuchin that America's trade actions against China were straining economic ties between the countries.

Chinese leaders contend that their country's economy is still developing. They openly reject Mr. Trump's call for reciprocity in trade relations. They have instead offered concessions like raising caps on foreign investors' stakes in Chinese financial institutions, and proposed eliminating import tariffs in narrow categories like drugs to treat cancer.

Beijing says that opening up some services sectors would improve the efficiency of the Chinese economy as well as make money for foreign companies. Improving health care, particularly for the aging, has also become a national priority.

But Chinese officials argue that their country is still dangerously reliant on smokestack industries of the past, like steel, aluminum and cheap manufacturing. The average Chinese household lives on a quarter of the income that American and Western European households do, and standards of living remain very low in rural parts of the country, and across central and western China.

Wang Shouwen, China's vice minister of commerce, and Pascal Lamy, a former director general of the World Trade Organization, squared off at the Beijing forum over precisely that issue.

Mr. Wang insisted that China had made considerable strides in opening up its health, agriculture and shipping sectors to international competition. He noted that the United States and the European Union had higher tariffs than China on some imports of shirts and dairy products. He argued that China meets its W.T.O. obligations; the W.T.O. has long allowed developing countries to have higher tariffs to protect certain industries from international competition.

Mr. Lamy, a longtime critic of protectionism and government intervention, dismissed those arguments. China — which has the world's second-largest economy, after the United States, and is the world's largest manufacturer by far, of everything from steel and cement to laptop computers — had made too much progress to be lumped in with poor countries, he said.

"Pretending it is like India, or like Senegal, or like Botswana is pushing the envelope too far," Mr. Lamy said. He added that China still had to do more to "ensure a level playing field between Chinese producers and foreign producers, whether they produce inside China or outside of China."

On crucial issues, China and the United States appear to be talking past each other, not even agreeing on what is being debated.

Take semiconductors, for example: China is a major customer for microchips, which are used to power computers, smartphones and an ever-widening array of other electronics. Chips from the United States account for just 4 percent of China's $260 billion in annual chip imports. While Chinese trade officials have been willing to discuss buying more chips from factories in the United States, that could take market share from Japan and South Korea. Washington has resisted that solution.

American officials say the problem is that China's national, provincial and municipal governments are working with state-owned banks to rush the construction of factories, particularly to make memory chips.

The new factories often rely on technology that foreign companies have had to transfer as a condition of competing in the Chinese market, according to the United States. Global trade rules ban mandatory technology transfers.

Numerous factories are nearing completion, which will unleash an avalanche of additional output. China contends that it has assisted the sector partly to upgrade its economy and partly because the factories will mainly be supplying its domestic market.

But since factories in China are the world's main assemblers of electronics, the country's drive for self-sufficiency in microchips could pose a threat to chip producers in the rest of the world.

For now, China seems to be pinning its hopes on heavy lobbying in Washington by Wall Street, traditionally Beijing's most reliable ally in bilateral disputes. China's sovereign wealth fund owns stakes in a variety of American financial institutions. Estimates of Chinese outbound investment over the next decade run as high as $2.5 trillion, a rich source of advisory fees in the United States.

Mr. Wang said on Sunday that China might go beyond its earlier offer to raise caps on foreign ownership in Chinese financial institutions. "It is even possible we will remove those caps altogether" in some categories, he said.

But he also made clear that China would not be intimidated if its offers are not enough to satisfy the Trump administration, which has focused on reviving American manufacturing.

"If China's interests are impaired," he said, "we will have to take measures."

# Economists Say U.S. Tariffs
# Are Wrong Move on a Valid Issue

BY JIM TANKERSLEY | APRIL 11, 2018

WASHINGTON — President Trump's advisers insist that the economics profession is solidly behind the administration's threat to impose tariffs on hundreds of billions of dollars of Chinese imports. Many top economists say, no, they're not.

Across the ideological spectrum, trade experts and former top economic advisers to presidents say Mr. Trump is right to highlight issues on which China is widely viewed as an offender, such as intellectual-property theft and access to its domestic market. But many of those experts say Mr. Trump's planned tariffs would backfire — by raising costs to American businesses and consumers, and by inviting retaliation against American exporters. They say he would better serve his purposes by enlisting international allies in a pressure campaign against Beijing.

"Many economists have said, yeah, there's some legitimate issues here," said Laura D. Tyson, an economist at the Haas School of Business of the University of California, Berkeley, who headed the Council of Economic Advisers under President Bill Clinton. "I haven't seen any who have said the appropriate response is a series of tariffs on a bunch of goods, most of which don't have any real link to the underlying issue."

Ms. Tyson and many other economists say it was mistake last year when Mr. Trump pulled the United States out of the Trans-Pacific Partnership. Proponents of that agreement say it would have unified a dozen countries against the Chinese on trade issues.

"I don't think the way the administration is going about it is a particularly strategic one," said David Autor, a Massachusetts Institute of Technology economist whose research suggests that opening trade with China cost the United States two million jobs in the late 1990s and early 2000s. "The first way to go about it should have been to sign TPP, which was set up as a bulwark against China."

Mr. Trump has long railed against Chinese trade practices, and he has long criticized previous presidents for their approach to the issue. This year, he has pushed aggressively on the issue. He levied tariffs on imported steel and aluminum that were largely viewed as a shot at Chinese oversupply of those metals. Then he proposed as much as $150 billion in tariffs on other imports from China.

His advisers have stressed that economists largely agree with Mr. Trump that the Chinese are stealing American intellectual property and restricting access to their market in ways that put American companies at a disadvantage.

"No free-market guy, no free-trade guy disagrees on this subject," Larry Kudlow, the new director of the National Economic Council, said on CNN's "State of the Union" on Sunday. "The guild, if you will, the brethren of the economic profession have all agreed that something has to be done."

Peter Navarro, the director of Mr. Trump's Office of Tade and Manufacturing Policy, told NBC's "Meet the Press" on Sunday that "what we have here is a situation where every American understands that China is stealing our intellectual property, they're forcing the transfer of our technology when companies go to China, and by doing that, they steal jobs from America, they steal factories from America, and we run an unprecedented $370-billion-a-year trade deficit in goods. This is an unsustainable situation."

Many economists agree that China needs to be confronted on several trade issues, though very few share Mr. Trump's fixation on the United States' trade deficit with China. Most say bilateral trade deficits are not a good measure of market access or the fairness of trade agreements.

"I think the basic issue that the Trump administration is pointing to — the lack of intellectual-property protection — is a serious one, particularly for the United States," said N. Gregory Mankiw, a

Larry Kudlow, above, and other presidential advisers have cited economists' support for the view that Chinese trade practices put American companies at an unfair disadvantage.

Harvard economist who headed President George W. Bush's Council of Economic Advisers. "It's a completely serious and appropriate issue for the administration to be concerned with."

What worries Mr. Mankiw and others is Mr. Trump's threat of tariffs, which administration officials have portrayed both as a bargaining chip and as a policy Mr. Trump would certainly carry through on.

Economic forecasters are just beginning to predict how tariffs would affect growth. Goldman Sachs analysts wrote this week that the currently proposed tariffs would cut less than 0.1 percentage points off American growth this year, but also said that "it is harder to rule out continued escalation to a level that does ultimately have a first-order impact on the economy" if the United States and China could not find compromise.

Because tariffs would raise prices for American businesses and consumers that buy imported goods, "you're hurting yourself if you follow through with it," Mr. Mankiw said. "It just seems to me to be a not very smart threat to be making, given that it would not be rational to follow through with it."

Economists who don't like tariffs but favor action against China largely say the United States should be forming a multinational coalition to confront the Chinese.

"Any good strategy has to include getting other countries on your side," said Jason Furman, an economist at Harvard's Kennedy School of Government who headed the Council of Economic Advisers under President Barack Obama. "If it's the United States versus China, we're similar-sized economies. If it's the United States and the world versus China, that's not something China can win."

Mr. Furman, Mr. Mankiw and others said the United States should continue to press its case against China before the World Trade Organization — a strategy that Mr. Navarro and other advisers to Mr. Trump say has not produced favorable results in the past. The economists who disagree with the administration's approach also stress, frequently, that joining the Trans-Pacific Partnership would have given the United States leverage in this dispute.

Since Mr. Trump quit the pact, 11 other countries have forged ahead on it. He said this year that he would reconsider joining the agreement if it was renegotiated to benefit the United States more substantially.

"It's obviously a terrible mistake" to have quit the agreement, said Austan Goolsbee, an economist at the University of Chicago's Booth School of Business and another past chairman of Mr. Obama's Council of Economic Advisers. "This was a coalition of the vast majority of the economies of Asia outside of China, agreeing to principles exactly of the form that we're now saying that we want. We would be in a lot better situation if we had all of those people on our side."

Mr. Trump's unilateral approach, including his tariff threats, has drawn qualified support from at least one unlikely high-profile economist: Martin Feldstein, of Harvard, a chairman of President Ronald Reagan's Council of Economic Advisers.

Mr. Feldstein began a syndicated op-ed column last month, on the subject of Mr. Trump's steel and aluminum tariffs, by declaring, "Like almost all economists and most policy analysts, I prefer low trade tariffs or no tariffs at all." But he went on to criticize China's intellectual-property policies and predict that the United States "cannot use traditional remedies for trade disputes or World Trade Organization procedures to stop China's behavior."

American negotiators, Mr. Feldstein wrote, would use tariff threats "as a way to persuade China's government to abandon the policy of 'voluntary' technology transfers."

"If that happens, and U.S. firms can do business in China without being compelled to pay such a steep competitive price," he continued, "the threat of tariffs will have been a very successful tool of trade policy."

# Chance of Nafta Deal in 2018 Diminishes as Talks Drag Past Congressional Deadline

BY ANA SWANSON AND ELISABETH MALKIN | MAY 17, 2018

WASHINGTON — The prospect of rewriting the North American Free Trade Agreement this year appeared to diminish significantly on Thursday, as a deadline set by congressional Republicans passed and the lead American trade negotiator, Robert Lighthizer, said the countries involved were "nowhere near close to a deal."

To get an agreement approved by the current, Republican-controlled Congress, Speaker Paul D. Ryan set a May 17 cutoff for the White House to notify Congress of an impending deal. As that deadline came and went on Thursday, Canada, Mexico and the United States

TODD SPOTH FOR THE NEW YORK TIMES

A pipe-threading plant in Texas. President Trump's trade representative said "gaping differences" on rewriting the North American Free Trade Agreement remained.

remained at odds over significant portions of the sprawling 24-year-old agreement.

Trade advisers across the political spectrum cautioned that the current Congress could still vote on the deal this year if negotiators wrapped up their talks in the next few weeks. But with significant disagreements remaining among the three countries as well as disparate views among the lawmakers who must approve the deal, the chance of Nafta's quick resolution is diminishing.

In a statement on Thursday, Mr. Lighthizer, the United States trade representative, said that "gaping differences" remained between the countries on intellectual property, agriculture, energy and other areas. "We of course will continue to engage in negotiations, and I look forward to working with my counterparts to secure the best possible deal for American farmers, ranchers, workers and businesses," he added.

The delays could leave the future of a revised Nafta in the hands of Democrats, if they win one or both houses of Congress in this year's midterm elections. And that in turn would most likely increase the chances that President Trump's Nafta deal would not be ratified by Congress at all, trade experts say.

Trump officials had been angling for a quick agreement to avoid that possibility and appeared to be making progress last week on key provisions related to automobiles. But the three countries have yet to finalize the auto terms and remain divided on some provisions, as well as other controversial points, like the Trump administration's proposal to add a five-year sunset clause to the deal and scale back legal protections for foreign investors.

Further complicating the talks is Mr. Trump's insistence that Mexico address the flow of migrants into the United States and his threat to tie immigration to the revised agreement.

American officials have proposed limiting the flow of migrants into the United States by creating what is known as a "Safe Third Country" agreement with Mexico. That would allow American border officials to turn away asylum seekers who use Mexico as a path to the United States.

The United States has such an agreement with Canada, and forging a similar pact with Mexico could significantly reduce the number of migrants flowing in over the southern border. But such a deal would create logistical and financial burdens for Mexico in dealing with asylum seekers, many of whom travel from Central America and through Mexico on their way to the United States.

Mexican officials — including the economy secretary, Ildefonso Guajardo, who is leading the Nafta talks — have insisted that the negotiations be confined to the content of the agreement itself, and not include immigration.

But the issues remain linked for Mr. Trump, who tweeted last month: "Mexico, whose laws on immigration are very tough, must stop people from going through Mexico and into the U.S. We may make this a condition of the new NAFTA Agreement."

Officials from both countries met on Thursday for the first of two days of scheduled talks on a range of issues related to immigration.

Sarah Huckabee Sanders, the White House press secretary, declined on Thursday to comment on continuing negotiations but said that, on immigration, "the president does want to see Mexico step up and do more."

Until last Friday, Mexican officials thought they had come to a compromise with their American counterparts on a key part of Nafta as they neared agreement on rules that would raise the share of an automobile's content that has to be made in the region to qualify for zero tariffs, and rules governing the minimum wages of those working on autos, according to a Mexican government official with knowledge of the talks.

The Mexicans have been eager to finalize an accord before their presidential election, which is scheduled for July 1. The Americans, believing the Mexicans would bend on the automobile rules to get a deal quickly, insisted on a toughened position last week and the Mexicans responded by rejecting the proposal, saying they would rather have no deal than a bad deal, according to officials briefed on the talks.

Michael C. Camuñez, a former official in the United States Commerce Department, said Mr. Lighthizer was pressing last week for the three countries to come to a separate agreement on the auto industry. In return, Mexico had expected flexibility on some points of contention, he said.

Mexican and Canadian negotiators insist that the Trump administration faces its toughest hurdles internally. Republicans now control both houses of Congress and could greatly accelerate or impede the ratification of a revised Nafta deal. But congressional Republicans, along with many business groups, oppose several of the Trump administration's signature proposals for overhauling Nafta, including the sunset clause and changes to investment rules.

The congressional calendar provides a short window for the current Congress to approve a revised pact. If Democrats take control of one or both chambers of Congress in the midterm elections, that could diminish the administration's chances of getting a vote at all.

Republicans are now urging the administration to come to a quicker resolution, which may require leaving some of those more difficult proposals on the cutting room floor.

"We'll see if they can get this done by May 17 and get us the paper to Congress," Mr. Ryan, Republican of Wisconsin, said on May 9. "Which then we could have this vote by December. If we can't, then we won't."

Representative Kevin Brady, the chairman of the powerful House Ways and Means Committee, reiterated those comments on Tuesday.

"We believe for the 115th Congress to vote this year on a new, modern Nafta, that this week is important for the negotiators to complete their work," said Mr. Brady, Republican of Texas. "So we're hopeful they'll continue to make progress on this agreement."

The pressure from congressional leaders may be an indication that they are losing their motivation to hold a vote this year.

Daniel Ikenson, the director of trade policy studies at the libertarian Cato Institute, said that if the administration notified Congress of its intent to sign a deal by the end of the month, that should be enough time for lawmakers to consider it in the lame duck session. He said Mr. Ryan's deadline was most likely an effort to get the Trump administration to pare back some of the demands that lawmakers think are not in the best interest of companies or workers.

"I think the best way for Trump to secure Republican support is just stop the charade, recognize you've made a go of it, maybe some things in the agreement will be updated, but it's time to stand down," Mr. Ikenson said. "I do think that's what Ryan and Republicans are hoping for."

Still, trade experts agree that the timeline for getting the colossal agreement through the current Congress is drawing uncomfortably close. And on June 1, the Trump administration's exemption for Canada and Mexico from the steel and aluminum tariffs will once again expire, adding another source of tension to the talks.

# Trump's Manchurian Trade Policy

OPINION | BY PAUL KRUGMAN | MAY 28, 2018

REMEMBER "The Manchurian Candidate"? The 1959 novel, made into a classic 1962 film (never mind the remake), involved a plot to install a Communist agent as president of the United States. One major irony was that the politician in question was modeled on Senator Joe McCarthy — that is, he posed as a superpatriot even while planning to betray America.

It all feels horribly relevant these days. But don't worry: This isn't going to be another piece on Donald Trump's collusion with Russia, which is being ably covered by other people. What I want to talk about instead are Trump's actions on international trade — which are starting to have a remarkably similar feel.

On one side, the "Make America Great Again" president is pursuing protectionist policies, supposedly in the name of national security, that will alienate many of our democratic allies. On the other side, he seems weirdly determined to prevent action against genuine national security threats posed by foreign dictatorships — in this case China. What's going on?

Some background: International trade is governed by a system of multinational agreements that countries are not supposed to break unilaterally. But when that system was created (under U.S. leadership) in 1947, its framers realized that it had to have a bit of flexibility, a few escape valves to let off political pressure. So nations were allowed to impose tariffs and other trade barriers under certain limited conditions, like sudden import surges.

Meanwhile, the U.S. created a domestic system of trade policy designed to be consistent with these international rules. Under that system, the White House can initiate investigations into possible adverse effects of imports and, if it chooses, impose tariffs or other measures on the basis of these investigations.

As I said, the conditions under which such actions are allowable are limited — with one big exception. Both the international rules and domestic law — Article XXI and Section 232, respectively — let the U.S. government do pretty much whatever it wants in the name of national security.

Historically, however, this national security exemption has been invoked very rarely, precisely because it's so open-ended. If the U.S. or any other major player began promiscuously using dubious national security arguments to abrogate trade agreements, everyone else would follow suit, and the whole trading system would fall apart. That's why there have been only a handful of Section 232 investigations over the past half century — and most of them ended with a presidential determination that no action was warranted.

But Trump is different. He has already imposed tariffs on steel and aluminum in the name of national security, and he is now threatening to do the same for autos.

The idea that imported cars pose a national security threat is absurd. We're not about to refight World War II, converting auto plants over to the production of Sherman tanks. And almost all the cars we import come from U.S. allies. Clearly, Trump's invocation of national security is a pretext, a way to bypass the rules that are supposed to limit arbitrary executive action.

And their economic side effects aside, the proposed auto tariffs would further undermine our allies' rapidly eroding faith in U.S. trustworthiness.

Which is not to say that national security should never be a consideration in international trade. On the contrary, there's a very clear-cut case right now: the Chinese company ZTE, which makes cheap phones and other electronic goods.

ZTE products include many U.S.-made high-technology components, some of which are prohibited from being exported to sanctioned regimes. But the company systematically violated these export rules, leading the Commerce Department to ban sales of those components to the company. And the Pentagon has banned sales of ZTE phones on U.S. military bases, warning that the phones could be used to conduct espionage.

Yet Trump is pulling out all the stops in an effort to reverse actions against ZTE, in defiance of lawmakers from both parties.

What's behind his bizarre determination to help an obvious bad actor? Is it about personal gain? China approved a huge loan to a Trump-related project in Indonesia just before rushing to ZTE's defense; at the same time, China granted valuable trademarks to Ivanka Trump. And don't say that it's ridiculous to suggest that Trump can be bribed; everything we know about him says that yes, he can.

And if we do have a president who's bribable, that's going to give dictators a leg up over democracies, which can't do that sort of thing because they operate under the rule of law.

Of course, there might be other explanations. Maybe President Xi Jinping told Trump that he needed to abase himself on this issue to get a trade deal he can call a "win." Somehow this doesn't sound much better.

Whatever the true explanation, what we're getting is Manchurian trade policy: a president using obviously fake national security arguments to hurt democratic allies, while ignoring very real national security concerns to help a hostile dictatorship.

# Trump Upends Global Trade Order Built by U.S.

BY ANA SWANSON | JUNE 10, 2018

WASHINGTON — At the rockiest annual meeting of major Western powers in decades, President Trump criticized the tariffs imposed on American goods as "ridiculous and unacceptable" and vowed to put an end to being "like a piggy bank that everybody is robbing."

Behind Mr. Trump's outrage is his belief that the United States is at a disadvantage when it comes to global trade and is on the losing end of tariffs imposed by other nations. But to many of the country's trading partners, the president's criticisms ring hollow given that the United States places its own tariffs on everything from trucks and peanuts to sugar and stilettos.

DOUG MILLS/THE NEW YORK TIMES

President Trump has criticized the tariffs imposed on American goods as "ridiculous and unacceptable."

"While the system has problems, it is in no way 'unfair,' to the U.S., which as a hegemon has set the rules and the exceptions to the rules," said Susan Aaronson, a professor at George Washington University's Elliott School of International Affairs.

The United States has long been the biggest champion of global trade, viewing the opening of borders as essential to strengthening not only its economy but the global economy as well. It led the way in building the international trading order in the 20th century, rising to become the world's predominant economy. Tariffs were used as a way to offer protection for certain industries, but free trade was considered the tide that would lift all boats because all countries involved would benefit.

Instead of viewing trade as a mutually beneficial relationship, the president has described trading relationships as a zero-sum game, in which the United States loses out when other countries have more favorable terms. Mr. Trump has seized on trade policy to prop up industries that he has promised to revitalize, such as manufacturing, by limiting foreign competition.

Many of the United States' tariffs were put in place to protect influential industries that lobbied the government to set high barriers to foreign products, including a 25 percent tariff on sugar and foreign trucks, and a 163 percent tariff on imported peanuts.

Mr. Trump has singled out specific products where American producers face barriers, like Canada's 270 percent tariff on imported milk and Europe's 10 percent tariffs on American cars. On Saturday night, as Mr. Trump left the Group of 7 summit meeting en route to Singapore for a meeting with North Korea, he lashed out at Prime Minister Justin Trudeau of Canada once again for his country's dairy tariffs and for his criticisms of Mr. Trump's trade measures.

"Very dishonest & weak," Mr. Trump wrote in a tweet aboard Air Force One. "Our Tariffs are in response to his of 270% on dairy!"

But on average, American tariffs are on par with those of other rich, developed countries, which tend to be low, according to the World Bank and the United Nations.

Among the developed nations that make up the Group of 7 that met in a resort town near Quebec City this weekend, the United States has tariffs that are slightly higher, on average, across all its imported products than Canada or Japan and exactly equivalent to the four European nations in the G-7.

So far this year, Mr. Trump has imposed tariffs on nearly $60 billion of steel, aluminum, solar products and washing machines that flow into the United States from around the world.

He is threatening additional tariffs on foreign goods that would expand his trade penalties significantly, including a tariff on $350 billion of imported automobiles and parts and levies on $150 billion worth of Chinese goods, on the assumption those will force trading partners to drop their own barriers to entry.

The approach risks upending the United States' longstanding embrace of free trade and its use of trading relationships to help power economic growth in the United States and the world economy writ large.

Since the Second World War, the United States has cut its tariff rates in step with other developed countries. It also gave some less-developed countries access to its markets, with the idea of increasing wages and improving quality of life.

Mr. Trump appears ready to change that equation and increasingly views every country as a threat, regardless of its economic strength.

Critics fear Mr. Trump's approach will hurt developing nations and result in an escalating series of tariffs that raise costs for American consumers and industries, potentially harming the very manufacturers Mr. Trump says his trade policy is intended to protect.

"Trump's bull in a china shop act is clearly grating on other trading partners, who now see the U.S. as a recalcitrant and unruly member of the global trading system rather than as a responsible steward," said Eswar Prasad, a professor of international trade at Cornell University. He said allies' tolerance had waned to a point "where they are more likely to retaliate and escalate trade disputes rather than give in to U.S. demands."

The president has reserved his harshest criticisms for Canada — the largest destination for American exports, and one of the United States' most open trading relationships under the terms of the 25-year-old North American Free Trade Agreement.

Mr. Trump has been angered in recent months by Canada's refusal to give in to his demands for rewriting Nafta and has consistently threatened to withdraw from the agreement. On Sunday, Mr. Trump's top economic adviser, Larry Kudlow, called the timing of Mr. Trudeau's criticism of the United States tariffs "a betrayal."

The president and his supporters argue that the United States must be willing to take drastic action to fulfill Mr. Trump's promise to rewrite trade agreements to protect American workers — a vow that found favor with many American workers and helped fuel his rise to the White House.

"The global trading system needs major surgery and every country must be part of the solution, even our friends," said Daniel DiMicco, a

DOUG MILLS/THE NEW YORK TIMES

President Trump with Prime Minister Justin Trudeau of Canada at the G-7 summit meeting. Mr. Trump has lashed out at Mr. Trudeau for his country's dairy tariffs.

former trade adviser to Mr. Trump's campaign and current chairman of the Coalition for a Prosperous America trade group.

Still, it is unclear whether Mr. Trump's approach will convince trading partners to make the concessions he wants.

Smaller countries like South Korea and Argentina have forged agreements with the United States in recent months. Last week, Brazil put into place the take-it-or-leave-it agreement the United States demanded to avoid Mr. Trump's 25 percent steel tariffs by limiting exports of finished steel into the United States.

But the world's major powers have so far responded to the president's criticisms by toughening their resolve. Indeed, Chancellor Angela Merkel of Germany said Sunday that Europe would enact countermeasures against the United States tariffs on steel and aluminum.

"When you go up and slap someone in the face, they're not going to say, 'Please sir, can I have another?' " said Philip Levy, a senior fellow at the Chicago Council on Global Affairs.

At a news conference on Saturday, Mr. Trump said his ultimate goal was eliminating all trade duties and subsidies. But in his short tenure in office, he has scrapped potential agreements like the Trans-Pacific Partnership with Japan and Canada and a sweeping trade pact with Europe that would have slashed the tariffs he is now criticizing.

The United States has just one trade agreement with the countries of the G-7 — Nafta, which includes Canada. The remaining countries of the group have recently inked multiple deals among themselves that have left American exporters at a disadvantage in their markets.

In the last year, a trade agreement between Canada and the European Union went into force, and remaining countries of the Trans-Pacific Partnership signed a trade pact, as did the European Union and Japan.

Mr. Trump's advisers have criticized these as bad deals, and argued that his "America First" strategy did not mean "America alone." But with the world's other leading economies moving ahead with trade pacts and united against Mr. Trump's trade approach, the United States certainly appears to be at odds with many of its former partners.

"The president's principal objection to multilateralism seems to be that he doesn't want other countries united against him," said Mr. Levy. "Now, look at what he's done."

# CHAPTER 2

# America First?

One of the themes of Donald Trump's 2016 presidential campaign was "America First," and a promise to make American manufacturing stronger and keep more jobs in the country. As president, Trump maintained that America was being treated unfairly by its trading partners, and that only by putting tariffs in place and changing established trading relationships would the U.S. be able to reap the benefits of those promises. These measures are meant to make America's interests come first, despite the repercussions.

## Trump Pitches 'America First' Trade Policy at Asia-Pacific Gathering

BY JULIE HIRSCHFELD DAVIS AND MARK LANDLER | NOV. 10, 2017

DANANG, VIETNAM — President Trump on Friday vowed to protect American interests against foreign exploitation, preaching a starkly unilateralist approach to a group of leaders who once pinned their economic hopes on a regional trade pact led by the United States.

"We are not going to let the United States be taken advantage of anymore," Mr. Trump told business leaders at the Asia-Pacific Economic Cooperation forum in Danang, Vietnam. "I am always going to put America first, the same way that I expect all of you in this room to put your countries first."

But taking the stage at the same meeting immediately after Mr. Trump, President Xi Jinping of China delivered a sharply contrasting message, championing more robust engagement with the world. Mr. Xi used his own speech to make a spirited defense of globalization, saying relations among countries should be "more open, more inclusive, more balanced, more equitable and more beneficial to all."

Mr. Trump's remarks were strikingly hostile for an audience that included leaders who had supported the Trans-Pacific Partnership, a sweeping 12-nation accord that was to be led by the United States, from which Mr. Trump withdrew immediately after taking office.

And it indicated the degree to which, under Mr. Trump, the United States — once a dominant voice guiding discussions about trade at gatherings such as APEC — has ceded that role. Even as he was railing against multilateral approaches, the remaining 11 countries in the Trans-Pacific Partnership were negotiating intensively to seal the agreement — without the United States. Under the terms being discussed, the United States could re-enter the pact in the future.

Even without the United States, the Trans-Pacific Partnership would be the largest trade agreement in history. Under the partnership, members would enjoy tariff-free trade with each other, with companies in the member countries having faster and better access to other markets than their American rivals.

Promising to pursue "mutually beneficial commerce" through bilateral trade agreements, Mr. Trump roundly condemned the kind of multilateral accords his predecessors had pursued. His talk echoed his statements in China earlier this week that blamed weak American leadership for trade imbalances that he said had stripped jobs, factories and entire industries from the United States.

"What we will no longer do is enter into large agreements that tie our hands, surrender our sovereignty and make meaningful enforcement practically impossible," Mr. Trump said.

He also spoke witheringly about an approach he said had led the United States to lower its own trade barriers, only to have other countries refuse to do so, and he accused the World Trade Organization of treating the United States unfairly.

Many of the president's toughest lines — his vow to fight the "audacious theft" of intellectual property from American companies and the forced transfer of technology to foreign firms — were aimed at China.

But Mr. Trump avoided criticizing Mr. Xi personally. And he repeated his contention that he did not blame China, or any other country, for taking advantage of what he called weak American trade laws.

"If their representatives are able to get away with it, they are just doing their jobs," the president said. "I wish previous administrations in my country saw what was happening and did something about it. They did not, but I will."

White House officials had framed Mr. Trump's speech as a chance to articulate the idea of a "free and open Indo-Pacific" region, which the Trump administration has adopted as its answer to former President Barack Obama's pivot to Asia. First proposed by the Japanese, it envisions the United States strengthening ties with three other democracies in the region — Australia, India and Japan — in part to counter a rising China. But the president offered few details about that approach.

He spoke of the need for freedom of navigation — a reference to the South China Sea, which Vietnam, Malaysia and other countries complain Beijing is turning into a private waterway. But the president stopped short of calling out China by name.

He also did not fault China or his host, Vietnam, for their checkered human rights records, even as he offered a general endorsement of the rule of law and individual rights.

As in his speech to the United Nations in September, Mr. Trump emphasized the idea of sovereignty, a concept that is often seen as being at odds with global cooperation and that is sometimes used by countries to fend off interference by outside powers.

He closed the speech with an inward-looking paean to the virtues of home, declaring, "In all of the world, there is no place like home," adding that nations should "protect your home, defend your home, and love your home today and for all time."

Mr. Xi, in contrast, argued for pursuing the kinds of global initiatives that Mr. Trump had shunned. The Chinese leader praised the Paris climate accord, called globalization an "irreversible historical trend" and said China would continue to pursue a free trade area in the Asia-Pacific region.

American and Russian officials had been working to arrange a meeting between President Vladimir V. Putin and Mr. Trump on the sidelines of the meeting, in part to ask for Moscow's assistance in countering the threat from North Korea. But as Mr. Trump arrived in Danang, the White House announced that he would not hold formal talks with Mr. Putin.

Officials cited scheduling issues as the reason the two leaders would not meet. But on Thursday, Rex W. Tillerson, the secretary of state, had said that a conversation between Mr. Trump and Mr. Putin was "still under consideration," and that a final decision would hinge on whether there was "sufficient substance" to warrant face-to-face talks.

Mr. Trump's last encounter with Mr. Putin — on the sidelines of the Group of 20 summit meeting in Hamburg, Germany — posed political challenges for the White House, which faced questions about whether and how sharply Mr. Trump would rebuke his Russian counterpart for meddling in the 2016 elections.

Mr. Trump was later criticized for not having pressed Mr. Putin more strongly in an hourslong meeting on the election interference, and for revelations that the two had a second, undisclosed discussion at a leaders' dinner that night. Diplomats described being stunned to see the two presidents chatting intimately with only a Kremlin interpreter present.

The optics of a meeting this week would have been particularly tricky, given new revelations about the Trump campaign's contacts with Russians, brought to light by the investigations into Moscow's efforts to sway the American election in Mr. Trump's favor.

The two presidents did end up shaking hands and exchanging greetings before posing for a photograph at the APEC gala dinner Friday evening.

Still, the change in plans appeared to have left the Kremlin exasperated. Asked about the absence of a meeting, Sergey V. Lavrov, the Russian foreign minister, told a Russian TV reporter: "Ask the Americans. We are not speaking on this matter at all."

Mr. Lavrov noted that Mr. Trump himself had said last week that he would most likely meet with Mr. Putin during his trip to Asia. But, Mr. Lavrov added, "I don't know what his bureaucrats are saying."

# Trump's Trade Policy Is Lifting Exports. Of Canadian Lobster.

BY ANA SWANSON  |  *NOV. 12, 2017*

CENTREVILLE, NOVA SCOTIA — This lobster factory on a windswept bay in eastern Canada is so remote that its workers have to drive for miles just to get cellphone service. But Gidney Fisheries is truly global, with its lobsters landing on plates in Paris and Shanghai through trade agreements hammered out in far-off capitals.

Of late, these trade pacts have been shifting in the factory's favor, giving it an advantage over its American competitors.

A new trade agreement between Canada and the European Union has slashed tariffs on imports of Canadian lobsters. That means more 747s filled with Christmas-red crustaceans will depart from Nova Scotia for European markets this winter — and more revenue will flow to Gidney Fisheries. The factory, which in the 1800s sent its lobsters to Boston by steamship, is flush with potential as it gains access to new markets and plans to increase its work force by roughly 50 percent, adding dozens of positions to its current payroll of around 85 workers.

"For us, free trade is a good thing," said Robert MacDonald, the president of Gidney Fisheries, which processes 10,000 to 15,000 lobsters a day.

The Trump administration has adopted a skeptical view of trade deals, promising to scrap or renegotiate global agreements that it believes put American companies and workers at a disadvantage. Among them is the North American Free Trade Agreement, which the United States is trying to renegotiate. It will join its partners in the agreement, Canada and Mexico, for a fifth round of talks in Mexico City that officially begin on Friday.

Some trade experts, though, say America's get-tough approach is dissuading foreign partners from jumping into talks. Other countries, like Canada, are forging ahead with their own trade deals as they

A high-tech machine allows Gidney Fisheries to extract the meat when it's raw.

balk at the tough terms the United States is demanding in its trade negotiations. Over the weekend, a group of 11 countries including Canada announced that they were committed to moving ahead with the Trans-Pacific Partnership, a sweeping multinational trade deal negotiated by the Obama administration.

As these deals progress, American companies, particularly exporters, are finding themselves on the losing end of global trade as their competitors abroad gain easier access to foreign markets.

"We live in such a low-margin world, where industry after industry is engaged in fierce global competition," said John G. Murphy, senior vice president for international policy at the U.S. Chamber of Commerce. "There is a sense in which the United States is standing still, while countries around us are moving forward."

It's a historic shift for the United States, which has long led the charge for free trade and open markets. The United States has traditionally been the global leader in forging trade pacts, including during

STEPHANIE FODEN FOR THE NEW YORK TIMES

Robert MacDonald, the president of Gidney Fisheries, with a catch. "For us, free trade is a good thing," he said.

the Obama administration, which negotiated an earlier version of the Trans-Pacific Partnership and began talks with Europe on an agreement known as the Trans-Atlantic Trade and Investment Partnership. Skeptics in the current administration criticize these pacts as a global race to the bottom that has cost American jobs and depressed wages. President Trump condemned the Trans-Pacific Partnership as one of the worst deals ever negotiated and officially withdrew the United States from the pact on his fourth day in office. Talks with Europe over the trans-Atlantic trade pact have stalled.

When Americans think about lobster, Maine often comes to mind. But Nova Scotia has emerged as a fierce competitor in exporting lobsters, particularly to Europe. Last year, American lobstermen sold only slightly more to Europe than their Canadian counterparts.

That balance could soon shift given the Canadian-European trade pact, which eliminated an 8 percent European tariff on live lobster when it went into effect in September. Tariffs on frozen and processed

Canadian lobster will be phased out in the next three to five years as part of the agreement.

The elimination of European tariffs is "the single most challenging issue" for the American lobster industry, said Annie Tselikis, the executive director of the Maine Lobster Dealers' Association, which represents companies that buy lobster from Maine fishermen. "This trade agreement does give Canada a huge leg up in the European marketplace," she said.

Ms. Tselikis said the pact was encouraging American companies to invest in new facilities in Canada to qualify for the lower European tariff.

"If the argument is you're not going to develop this trade policy because you're worried about outsourcing jobs — well, here we are, potentially outsourcing jobs due to an absence of trade policy," she said.

Gidney Fisheries, which exports live and frozen lobster, is poised to take advantage of the changing terms of trade. Last year, in anticipation of increased demand, the factory invested in state-of-the-art technology to set itself apart.

The company imported a German machine, sometimes used to make cold-pressed juice, that creates pressure of up to 87,000 pounds per square inch. The machine compresses the lobster in its shell, breaking the connective tissue, killing the lobster in seconds and allowing the meat to be extracted entirely raw — a selling point for chefs and consumers, as the process is considered relatively humane.

On the factory floor in September, a worker in a gray smock covered by a shiny rubber apron loaded lobsters into a plastic tube to feed into the machine. A dozen workers smashed claws, used tiny air hoses to remove entrails and sorted peachy-pink lobster meat into various packages to be flash frozen.

"A decade or two ago, there would be very few players who would have been shipping internationally," Mr. MacDonald said. "We now ship live lobsters all over the world."

The factory plans to add dozens of jobs now that a new trade deal has slashed European tariffs on Canadian lobsters.

Once mostly confined to the plates of the rich, lobster has gone mass market. A glut in the global catch roughly five years ago — the product of overfishing cod, a natural lobster predator — caused the price to plummet. Lobster rolls and lobster mac and cheese suddenly appeared on menus of fast food chains like Pret a Manger, Au Bon Pain, Quiznos and even McDonald's locations in New England.

Better packaging and faster freight services allowed American and Canadian exporters to expand into Europe and Asia. Exporters found a promising new market in China, where newly affluent diners were eagerly adopting Western luxury products like wine, caviar and lobster as a marker of taste and distinction.

Gidney Fisheries sought to tap into that market, with the help of Duan Zeng, Mr. MacDonald's colleague. Ms. Zeng, who has a master's degree in fish biology, does much of her work on WeChat, a Chinese mobile app, where she sells its wares. Last December, the company teamed up with Alibaba, the Chinese e-commerce company, to sell premium lobsters online.

Gidney Fisheries' largest market by far is still the United States, where the company supplies restaurants and hotel chains with Nova Scotia lobsters. But given the changing dynamics of trade pacts, Europe could soon be its fastest-growing market, much to the chagrin of American lobstermen, who were hopeful the United States would sign its own agreement with the European Union.

The Trump administration has not said whether it will continue trade talks with Europe. But other trade pacts under discussion, including Nafta, have shown little progress. In mid-October, Jyrki Katainen, a high-ranking European Union official, said Europe was "negotiating with all Nafta countries, and with all TPP countries, except one" — a not-so-veiled reference to America.

John Weekes, Canada's Nafta negotiator in the 1990s, said he initially believed Canadian companies might have just a narrow window of advantage over their American competitors. Now, that window looks quite a bit larger.

"It does open up a number of opportunities for Canadians that clearly aren't going to be available to Americans in the foreseeable future," Mr. Weekes said.

# Trump Says He Made Up Deficit Claim in Talk with Trudeau, Baffling Canadians

BY IAN AUSTEN AND DAN BILEFSKY | MARCH 15, 2018

OTTAWA — First were the tariffs on Canadian softwood lumber. Then came a trade action over a Canadian jetliner, and duties on newsprint. Most recently the United States and Canada battled over potentially crippling duties on steel and aluminum that President Trump introduced last week.

And all along the two countries have been fighting over renegotiations of the North American Free Trade Agreement.

Now comes the latest slight to Canada from its closest ally and nearest neighbor: a report by The Washington Post on Thursday that Mr. Trump boasted at a private fund-raising event that he made up an assertion that the United States had a trade deficit with Canada during a meeting with Prime Minister Justin Trudeau.

Trade with the United States is a critical part of Canada's export-dependent economy, and the actions and statements from the Trump administration concerning the two countries' economic relationship have provoked equal parts anxiety, puzzlement and anger within Canada.

The president's reported comments dominated the news in Canada on Thursday morning and were greeted with bafflement by some Canadians.

"I thought it was a dumb comment but I wasn't surprised," said Mark Warner, an international trade lawyer in Toronto. "If it came from any other world leader it would be troubling. But pretty obviously he's not a details guy and he's kind of got a negotiating strategy of being in the moment."

President Trump boasted at a fund-raising event on Wednesday that he fabricated a trade deficit between Canada and the United States during a meeting with Prime Minister Justin Trudeau.

In Quebec, where Mr. Trump's aggressive trade tactics, protectionist impulses and "America First" mantra have been met with concern and bemusement, Canadians were not impressed by what some construed as just the latest example of "lies" and obfuscation by Mr. Trump.

"It is scary, as his lying has become the new normal," said Cory Whiteduck, a 35-year-old radio host and cigarette seller in Kitigan Zibi reserve, near Maniwaki, Quebec, about 85 miles north of Ottawa. "Normally it would raise red flags, and a politician would be in trouble. It is not a productive way of doing things or a good mentality."

Michel Pronovost, a retired construction worker, said Mr. Trudeau was, by now, accustomed to Mr. Trump's creativity with the facts.

"Do you really think he didn't know that Trump was lying to him?" he asked. "Of course, he knew." But he added that while Mr. Trump's protectionism was bad for Canada, he was "trying to protect his own people, just like China or any country would do."

Some Americans denounced Mr. Trump's admission, including Bruce A. Heyman, the United States' ambassador to Canada under President Barack Obama, who spoke out in a series of posts on Twitter.

"Creating a crisis where none existed before is no way to run our country," Mr. Heyman posted. "Canada is our best friend and don't ever forget it! We should never put the relationship at risk."

He added: "When I left it was the best relationship the U.S.A. had in the world. The President is casually throwing Canada under the bus and this is just wrong."

Determining trade balances is not straightforward. According to the United States trade office, the United States had a $12.1 billion deficit in the trade in goods with Canada in 2016. But that was more than offset by a $24.6 billion surplus in the United States' favor in trade in services.

In a statement, the Canadian government noted the United States trade representative's finding of a surplus. Mr. Trudeau's office declined to comment.

On Thursday morning, Mr. Trump was not backing down. On Twitter he wrote: "We do have a Trade Deficit with Canada, as we do with almost all countries (some of them massive). P.M. Justin Trudeau of Canada, a very good guy, doesn't like saying that Canada has a Surplus vs. the U.S. (negotiating), but they do … they almost all do … and that's how I know!"

Trade disputes between Canada and the United States have not run a straight course. After Washington introduced the duties on steel and aluminum, it suspended them for Canada.

But officials in Mr. Trump's administration insist that the United States runs a steel trade deficit with Canada, even though figures from both governments show that trade is balanced.

The trade action over the new Canadian jetliner was ultimately dropped, but not before threatening the future of Bombardier, one of Canada's largest industrial companies.

After demanding that the North American Free Trade Agreement be reopened, Mr. Trump's negotiators presented a list of demands that Canada has declared unacceptable. Mr. Trudeau has said that Canada is prepared to abandon Nafta rather than accept a "bad deal."

# 'It's Factory North America,' but Trump Could Hobble It

BY ANA SWANSON | MARCH 30, 2018

CHICAGO — If North America were a factory, Union Pacific would be its biggest conveyor belt.

Based in Omaha, the company operates the largest rail network on the continent, a conduit that provides us with cereal, lumber, car parts and pretty much everything that touches our lives. That makes the railroad a real-time barometer of the fluctuations in global trade — a physical manifestation of how President Trump's agenda to remake the rules of commerce will play out.

Roughly 40 percent of the goods that Union Pacific moves touch an international border at some point in their journey, putting the railroad at the center of the global tensions that have arisen as the

WHITTEN SABBATINI FOR THE NEW YORK TIMES

A Union Pacific train departing from the terminal in Joliet, Ill.

administration prepares to impose tariffs on goods from China and steel and aluminum from around the world. Seventy percent of rail freight between the United States and Mexico travels on Union Pacific trains, meaning the outcome of the tense renegotiations for the North American Free Trade Agreement will shape the company's future.

"At its guts, a railroad like Union Pacific is built on people consuming stuff, industry consuming stuff, and trade flows," said Lance Fritz, Union Pacific's chief executive. "When those are happening and growing, we thrive. And all of that potentially gets impacted by getting Nafta wrong or the United States exiting Nafta."

These global forces all converge outside Chicago, where six of the seven largest railroads operating in the United States meet, including Union Pacific, Norfolk Southern and Canadian National. Here, roughly 300 workers move containers of barbecue grills, soybeans and socks from trains to trucks. Some of those trucks head out on the nearby tangle of interstate highways for multiday trips across the country. Some drive for Rust Belt factories or nearby warehouses for Walmart and Dollar Tree.

Union Pacific was created in 1862, when Abraham Lincoln ordered the company to open the American West by helping to build the first transcontinental railroad. Over the decades since, the company chiseled new rail lines out of impassable terrain and swallowed up its competitors. Today, the company's trains run on tracks it owns throughout 23 states west of the Mississippi River, and on partner networks in the Eastern United States, Canada and Mexico.

The company's financial history is inextricably tied to the country's economic ebbs and flows. Union Pacific saw its beef shipments fall in 2003, after an outbreak of mad cow disease in the United States prompted China to ban imports of American beef. In 2012, a drought shrank the company's wheat shipments and its revenues from agriculture.

In 1994, the introduction of Nafta slashed tariffs on products and encouraged companies to invest in supply chains stretching across

Union Pacific moves more than 100 carloads of beer from Mexico to the United States every day, with each carrying enough beer to provide an American consumer with a daily six-pack for 43 years.

borders — increasing rail traffic around North America. The year after Nafta went into effect, Mexico privatized its railroads, creating private commercial partners south of the border.

In 1999, Union Pacific had $700 million in business going to and from Mexico. Today, that figure has ballooned to more than $2.2 billion, with goods like grain and auto parts going into Mexico and finished cars, avocados and televisions coming back.

The company moves more than 100 carloads of beer from Mexico to the United States every day, with each carrying enough beer to provide an American consumer with a daily six-pack for 43 years.

To satisfy a changing diet, Union Pacific is introducing more refrigerated cars to carry meat into Mexico. The company is also investing $550 million on a massive rail yard in Texas that will help serve as a conduit for cross-border trade.

Now the fate of Nafta — and Union Pacific's business — is up in the air. All three countries are locked in contentious talks. American trade negotiators have said they believe they are close to completing a deal, though Mr. Trump continues to threaten to withdraw from the pact.

"Effectively, it's factory North America, and the administration is threatening to build a wall in the middle of the factory," said Emily Blanchard, an associate professor at the Tuck School of Business at Dartmouth College who studies trade.

Mr. Fritz has lobbied hard to preserve Nafta, submitting comments to the government about the pact's importance, writing opinion pieces and meeting with members of both Congress and the Trump administration. The company is exposed to almost every change the president has proposed, like requiring more of an automobile to be made in the United States and weakening the systems for settling disputes between countries.

"Capital investment is the lifeblood of an economy," Mr. Fritz said. He added that the Trump administration's proposals would be "the equivalent of killing foreign investment in our economies."

The railroad is also bracing for tariffs on steel and aluminum that went into effect March 23, as well as a new round of coming levies on products imported from China.

The railroad could see business pick up if American mills start cranking out more metals as foreign competition ebbs — or it could face a decline from industries, like automobiles, that will see their steel and aluminum costs rise. If the Trump administration follows through on tariffs on Chinese products, the tariffs will raise costs and slow sales for a wide variety of goods on the shelves of Walmart and Target.

And if China and other countries retaliate against these trade measures by making it more expensive for American companies to sell products like soybeans, pork and whiskey overseas, as they have threatened to, that, too, would mean less cargo for Union Pacific.

The company expects its own costs to increase as a result of the tariffs. Union Pacific uses American steel in its railroad cars, locomotives and some of its tracks. But on its most heavily trafficked lines — like its main east-west lines that run from Omaha to San Francisco and California to Texas — it opts for more expensive, ultra-hard rail made by Japan's Nippon Steel.

While many American allies were granted exemptions from the steel tariffs, Japan so far has not. That Japanese steel, which Union Pacific said is not matched in the United States, is now subject to a 25 percent tariff when it enters the country. Union Pacific is planning to ask the government for a special exemption for the product.

While Mr. Fritz said he understood the administration's desire to ensure that trade is fair, he doesn't believe tariffs are the answer.

"In general, they're going to raise the cost of production, or directly raise the cost to consumers," he said. "So neither is a good thing for the economy."

# Across Midwest, Farmers Warn of G.O.P. Losses Over Trump's Trade Policy

BY JONATHAN MARTIN | APRIL 18, 2018

CASSELTON, N.D. — Here in the largest soybean-producing county in the country, a snowy winter has left North Dakota farmers like Robert Runck with time on their hands before spring planting — time they have spent stewing over how much they stand to lose if President Trump starts a trade war with China.

"If he doesn't understand what he's doing to the nation by doing what he's doing, he's going to be a one-term president, plain and simple," said Mr. Runck, a fourth-generation farmer who voted for Mr. Trump. Pausing outside the post office in this town of 2,300, Mr. Runck said the repercussions could be more immediate for Representative Kevin Cramer, a Republican whose bid against Senator Heidi Heitkamp, a Democrat, has been complicated by the proposed tariffs.

"If it doesn't get resolved by election time, I would imagine it would cost Kevin Cramer some votes," he said.

Stern warnings are coming from all over the Midwest about the political peril for Republicans in Mr. Trump's recent course of action, in which the tariffs he slapped on foreign competitors invited retaliatory tariffs on American agriculture. Soybeans are America's second largest export to China, and that country's proposed 25 percent duties on the crop would hit hardest in states like Iowa, Kansas and Minnesota — where there are highly competitive House races — as well as Indiana, Missouri and North Dakota, whose Senate contests may determine control of the chamber.

By proposing the tariffs, Mr. Trump has moved to fulfill a central promise of his campaign: confronting those countries he believes are undermining American industry. Yet his goal — to revive the steel and aluminum industries, thereby aiding the Rust Belt states that were crucial to his election — has effectively prioritized one element of the Trump political coalition over another, larger bloc of voters. That larger segment, the farm belt, is essential to Republican success in the midterm elections and beyond.

From the still-thawing soybean fields of North Dakota and Kansas to the corn and pork farms of Iowa, voters across the political spectrum say the president's attacks on American economic rivals could do grave damage to an already unstable commodities market.

"They're not in touch with the reality of the Midwest and the impact that the tariffs would have," said Bart Bergquist, a biology professor and part-time farmer who lives on 10 acres just south of Waterloo, Iowa. Mr. Bergquist, who voted for Mr. Trump in the 2016 election, added that commodities prices had already taken a toll on the area.

"I know my neighbors are not rolling in money — they're trying to supplement whatever else they can do to keep going," he said.

Representative Rod Blum, a Republican, represents much of eastern Iowa and is facing a highly competitive race in what is the second-largest soybean-producing congressional district in the country. He and other politicians are facing a "nervous" farm community across the state, according to Grant Young, an Iowa-based Republican strategist.

"I listen to the farm show over the noon hour on WHO daily," Mr. Young said of Iowa's leading radio station. "They are usually a happy-go-lucky bunch promoting industry and holding a two-hour infomercial for the Farm Bureau. But the last couple of months I'm wondering if they need to take the sharp objects out of the studio."

In Kansas, Bob Henry, who grows corn and soybeans in another up-for-grabs House district near the Nebraska border, said the country could ill afford to tangle with a market that American farmers rely on.

"For the United States soybean grower, China is the 800-pound gorilla in the room," Mr. Henry said. He suggested that Beijing is exacting political payback against the Republican heartland: "China knows who got Trump elected."

After an initial round of tariffs on a modest share of American exports, the Chinese have displayed a more keen awareness of the electoral map and moved to punish those industries whose misfortune will be felt most intensely in states and districts pivotal in 2018.

Karl Rove, the former strategist to President George W. Bush, said a trade clash "would limit Midwestern enthusiasm from our base and limit our ability to hold what we have and pick up more seats." Mr. Rove also grumbled that Mr. Trump "has little to no understanding of the farm coalition."

He may have a slightly better appreciation after a meeting last week in the West Wing with a small group of farm belt Republican senators and governors, during which two of them brought up the adverse impact that tariffs on exports could have in the midterm election, according to officials briefed on the conversation.

Mr. Trump used the session to direct a pair of his top economic advisers to reconsider whether the United States should join a free-trade pact with a group of Pacific nations. But just hours later he signaled on Twitter that he was unlikely to reverse course on that agreement, the Trans-Pacific Partnership.

Instead, there are already whispers, in Washington and in agriculture states, that the president is risking a replay of President Jimmy Carter's grain embargo on the Soviets, which contributed to the massive losses Democrats suffered in 1980.

Indeed, after a year in which Mr. Trump only mused about pulling out of Nafta and was stymied by Congress in his attempt to slash the Agriculture Department's budget, there is now a sense in the farm belt that Mr. Trump's yearning to punish China could inflict real economic and political damage on his own political base.

"This is the first time it's in your face, especially to us in the Midwest," said Ed Schafer, a Republican former governor of North Dakota who was agriculture secretary under George W. Bush.

There may be no other race in America that is at once as significant as the Senate contest here and as shaped by whether China's tariffs take effect this year. Most of North Dakota's votes are in the eastern end of the state, in the Red River Valley — a region that also happens to be home to the three largest soybean-producing counties in the nation.

Senator Heitkamp won her seat by fewer than 3,000 votes in 2012. She remains personally popular, a valuable asset in a state with just 570,000 voters, but North Dakota has turned sharply away from Democrats in recent years.

But Mr. Trump has now handed her what may be a political gift.

"Senator Heitkamp will jump on the big, bad Trump and the stupid policy that's coming out of Washington hurting our farmers," Mr. Schafer said. "That's a strong message in North Dakota."

Or as Rob Port, a conservative talk radio host and columnist in the state, put it: "This is the perfect issue for her. Her base eats up the Trump bashing, but it's also an economic argument that'll have rural Trump voters saying, 'Maybe blind allegiance to Trump isn't such a good thing.' "

Ms. Heitkamp is already testing out such a message against her rival, Mr. Cramer.

"Clearly he sees his role is to be a vote for President Trump in the United States Senate," she said. "And I believe my role is to be a vote for North Dakota in the United States Senate."

Mr. Cramer, who Mr. Trump repeatedly wooed to run for the Senate, accused his opponent of "hysteria" and said she was overstating what are at this point only trade negotiations.

"People in North Dakota prefer humility to hyperbole, and that kind of hyperbole I don't think sells very well politically," he said. "But it's certainly not good for our farmers or good for our economy."

But on a local talk radio program, Mr. Cramer let slip his frustration with the president's actions. "He tends to have rather emotional responses," he said of Mr. Trump.

North Dakota is not simply another red state where Democrats are bound for extinction. There is an enduring populist streak here, dating back to its mistrust of distant bankers and millers in Minneapolis, Chicago and New York. To this day, the state retains a state-controlled bank and mill.

"We're Republicans until it comes to subsidies for farmers," said George Blank, only half-jokingly, as he sipped coffee with a half dozen fellow retirees at their daily breakfast-and-bull session in Casselton's Country Kitchen.

And, Mr. Blank noted, "everything drives on ag in this state."

Recalling his years running a construction supply business in a state where one in four jobs is agriculture-related, he said: "When the price of corn went down that impacted us greatly."

Now, though, soybeans have become the go-to commodity, said Vanessa Kummer, who farms 4,000 acres with her husband and son near Colfax, N.D. "It has become our cash crop and the most reliable crop to go to," she said.

Nancy Johnson, who leads the North Dakota Soybean Growers Association, reached for a measure of cheery, upper-Midwest optimism as she expressed hope that the threat of tariffs was merely "a negotiating tactic" by Mr. Trump. But Ms. Johnson, who wears a soybean pendant necklace, said her farmers "are rightly concerned, because we're being used as a weapon."

Over on William Hejl's farm in Amenia, N.D., just north of Casselton and part of the 86 percent of the state that is made up of farmland and ranches, the anxiety is as difficult to miss as the April snow crunching underfoot.

Showing a visitor his gleaming, green John Deere tractor, still in its shed for winter, Mr. Hejl said to "check back in August" — and not just to find better weather.

"If this thing hasn't been resolved, that's when it's going to hurt," he said of the outset of harvesting. "You've got to pay for the fuel and for the people to drive the combine."

Agriculture-dependent states like North Dakota went strongly for President Trump in 2016, but voters are also keenly concerned about trade. Casselton, N.D., is in the county that produces more soybeans than any other in the United States.

Kevin Skunes, a neighboring farmer who is also president of the National Corn Growers Association, joined Mr. Hejl and a visiting reporter for coffee, a brownie and a chance to sound the alarm.

"In an already depressed farm economy, if we take another hit on soybeans and corn it's going to be disastrous," Mr. Skunes said.

Back outside the post office in Casselton, Mr. Runck found his voice nearly drowned out by the sound of the speeding Burlington Northern Santa Fe — the same freight train that will be carrying crops west to the Pacific this fall.

But his answer carried clearly when he was asked whether he would support Ms. Heitkamp or Mr. Cramer: "I think the president has got to do the right thing between now and the election."

# Trump's Trade Moves Put U.S. Carmakers in a Jam at Home and Abroad

BY JIM TANKERSLEY AND ANA SWANSON | MAY 10, 2018

WASHINGTON — President Trump frequently talks about reviving the American auto industry, but his approach to trade policy may backfire on the country's carmakers.

Mr. Trump's efforts to renegotiate the North American Free Trade Agreement, to impose tariffs on imported aluminum and steel and to reduce America's trade deficit with China could limit the reach of companies that produce cars in the United States and depend on access to growing markets outside the country.

On Friday, the chief executives of the biggest automakers plan to meet with the president at the White House. The gathering comes at a critical moment, as Trump administration officials race to finalize a Nafta rewrite in the next few weeks and prepare to meet again next week with Chinese leaders in hopes of forestalling a potential trade war.

The auto industry is among the sectors most vulnerable to trade disruptions because its business model is increasingly global, in terms of both production and sales. One in five cars made in the United States is now exported, and one in four vehicles sold in America were produced in factories run by foreign-owned companies. General Motors sold nearly 1 million vehicles in China in the first quarter of the year — more than it sold in North America in the same period.

In the last two decades, United States automakers have set up plants in Canada, China and Mexico, and they routinely import car parts from other countries. Mexico has added hundreds of thousands of auto-making jobs since Nafta's enactment in 1994, while the United States has lost hundreds of thousands.

Labor groups and administration officials are hopeful that the trade moves will change incentives to encourage domestic and foreign-owned carmakers to manufacture more of their vehicles in the United States. But industry representatives warn that proposals now being championed by the Trump administration could have the opposite effect, raising the prices of American-made cars and trucks, reducing vehicle sales and potentially choking off access to China, the world's fastest-growing market for automobiles.

"There are so many fronts open that introduce risk into the autos' business, and the suppliers' business, that I don't know how you do any business planning at all right now," said Kristin Dziczek, vice president for industry, labor and economics at the Center for Automotive Research in Michigan. "They're playing with big money and big risk and big companies that employ a lot of people."

The biggest risk may relate to the rewriting of Nafta, a drawn-out process beset by disagreements between Canada, Mexico and the United States, and punctuated by Mr. Trump's repeated threat to withdraw from the deal if it is not revised in America's favor. Those threats have spooked automakers, whose fortunes are closely tied to the ways the accord has allowed them to reduce the cost of production and parts.

Negotiators have moved closer to agreement, but there are still big disagreements — particularly over the issue of auto manufacturing — that could scuttle the deal entirely or delay it so long that the Republican-controlled Congress is denied the opportunity to approve the revisions quickly.

One of the biggest sticking points relates to the portion of a car that must be made in North America to qualify for Nafta's zero tariffs. American automakers support high levels of North American production, but they do not want onerous requirements that prevent them from using products from Mexico or countries like China and Japan. Automakers have warned that the administration's demands would be expensive to comply with, and could push them to move some production out of North America altogether.

Administration officials initially demanded that 85 percent of a car's content come from North America, but they have dropped the requirement to 75 percent in the latest round of talks, which are going on this week. That is still above the current threshold of 62.5 percent and beyond the 70 percent level that Mexico is demanding.

Administration officials also want at least 40 percent of every vehicle to be manufactured by workers earning at least $16 an hour, a potential blow to Mexico, where wages are lower, that could benefit workers in the United States if it discouraged carmakers from shifting jobs to Mexico.

Ms. Dziczek and her colleagues at the automotive research center said that the proposed Nafta rule changes could subject 25 to 87 percent of vehicles sold in the United States to new tariffs, raising the price of those vehicles by $470 to $2,200 each. A report by the center warns that such increases would reduce annual auto sales in the United States by 60,000 to 150,000.

Manufacturing trade groups have warned about the risks of the administration's approach, but auto executives have stayed quiet publicly on trade issues, in part to avoid antagonizing officials in any of the countries that they depend on for sales.

"There is a lot of risk" for automakers in the current trade environment, said John Bozzella, a former Chrysler executive and the president and chief executive of the Association of Global Automakers, a Washington trade group for foreign-owned carmakers including Toyota and Nissan. "In all of these, you see the potential in raising production costs on vehicles built in the United States. And not just vehicles for trade."

The tariffs on steel (25 percent) and aluminum (10 percent) are also a looming threat to the automakers' profitability, given that American companies rely on products from countries like Japan and China that are not exempt from the levies. The Trump administration has temporarily exempted the European Union, Canada and Mexico from the tariffs until June 1, and officials have said they will only make the exemptions permanent if the affected countries voluntarily lower the amount of metals they export to the United States.

In 2017, the Ford Mustang, assembled in the United States, got 52 percent of its parts from the United States and Canada, according to statistics from the National Highway Traffic Safety Administration. The Dodge Charger, assembled in Canada, got nearly a quarter of its parts from Mexico, including the engines in some of its models, although the 3.6 liter version is made in the United States. The Honda Accord, which is assembled in the United States, includes 70 percent American and Canadian content, and 15 percent from Japan.

Asked about Mr. Trump's tariffs on an earnings call, Ford Motor's president and chief executive, James P. Hackett, said he had told world leaders that "what we crave as business people are certainty and equilibrium."

"So trade can thrive in a world where that's not in question," he continued.

"And so we have, like everyone, we're dealing with the sudden news, and I think we've done a great job internally of dealing with that."

But, he added, "We're not going to be victims in this kind of thing."

The trade showdown with China could pose an even greater risk to automakers, but it could also offer possibilities if resolved carefully. Car companies have long chafed under the rules they must heed to produce vehicles in China, including requirements that they enter into joint partnerships with Chinese companies. They have long urged China to reduce its 25 percent tariffs on imported vehicles, which President Xi Jinping promised to do in a speech last month.

Automakers would love to see Mr. Trump and his negotiating team win more concessions from the Chinese on those issues. Many of them also fear the opposite case: that in an escalating trade war, China could limit market access for foreign-owned automakers, choking off a key source of growth.

# Potential Auto Tariffs Prompt Warnings From Industry and Allies

BY ANA SWANSON AND JIM TANKERSLEY | MAY 24, 2018

WASHINGTON — President Trump likes to keep allies and adversaries guessing, but his decision to begin a trade investigation that could trigger auto tariffs was met by surprise at home and abroad, and prompted warnings that it could destabilize global supply chains.

Mr. Trump has argued that tariffs would encourage companies to move production back to American soil after years of offshoring and he has seized on levies as a way to force trading partners to make concessions, such as limiting exports to the United States.

But critics of Mr. Trump's approach say the president is sowing uncertainty that threatens to undercut economic growth and send trading relations to a previously unseen level of disarray.

Mr. Trump's latest tariff threat came Wednesday, in the middle of a series of foreign policy challenges: White House officials canceled a meeting with North Korea, drew the ire of lawmakers by considering easing penalties on a Chinese telecom firm and said they had secured a $200 billion trade concession with China, only to have the deal fall through.

But that wasn't all. This week, India filed formal challenges to Mr. Trump's steel and aluminum tariffs at the World Trade Organization, joining the European Union, Japan, Russia and Turkey.

Even members of the president's own party warned of the debilitating uncertainty businesses are facing from his scattershot approach.

"You pass a permanent tax reform for corporations and say, let's do business in America," said Douglas Holtz-Eakin, the president of the American Action Forum, a conservative-leaning think tank, and a former director of the Congressional Budget Office. "And then every day, you don't know which of your goods will have a tariff wall around it. It makes no sense."

The president has often vowed to defend and strengthen American manufacturing, but some critics believe that he doesn't take into account the complex web of materials and components that are sourced from around the world.

Promises to shake up American trade were a mainstay for the president on the campaign trail, and the idea of auto tariffs graced the trade to-do list on the white board in the office of the former White House adviser Steve Bannon in the early months of the administration. On Thursday, the United Autoworkers President Dennis Williams was cautiously optimistic about the president's decision to examine auto imports on national security grounds. Mr. Williams said he believed the United States should have been looking into imports long ago.

But beyond the president's base, the threat of tariffs on cars, trucks, S.U.V.s and auto parts appeared to provoke alarm from nearly every corner, with warnings that it would ultimately hurt American workers and consumers more than anyone else.

"If this proposal is carried out, it would deal a staggering blow to the very industry it purports to protect and would threaten to ignite a global trade war," said Thomas J. Donohue, the president of the U.S. Chamber of Commerce.

Senator Patrick J. Toomey, Republican of Pennsylvania, blasted the potential for tariffs on imported vehicles as a "bad idea," and added, "This is a dangerous course and should be abandoned immediately."

The administration authorized the investigation under the same legal statute it used to impose tariffs on steel and aluminum imports in March. As with that action, the Commerce Department on Wednesday said imported vehicles may pose a national security threat because they had degraded American manufacturing and put domestic technological development at risk.

But many find the national security argument specious. Roughly 44 percent of cars, trucks and S.U.V.s sold in the United States last year were imported, but 98 percent of American car imports came from major allies, like Canada, Mexico, the European Union, Japan and South Korea.

And while Mr. Trump wants to punish imports, the nature of car manufacturing means that tariffs could affect products even if they were largely made in America or made by American companies. The supply chains of both American and foreign branded cars crisscross international borders, and all the major brands use a variety of parts sourced from abroad, even if the vehicles are assembled in the United States. The Chevrolet Suburban, for example, draws a larger share of its parts from Mexico than from the United States and Canada combined, according to the National Highway Traffic Safety Administration.

Chrystia Freeland, the Canadian foreign minister, said that the idea that there could be a national security threat posed by cars and car parts from Canada — many of which cross the border multiple times in their journey from the factory to the customer — was "frankly absurd."

"That is a point that we are making very clearly to our U.S. partners and allies," she said.

Margaritas Schinas, the senior spokesman for the European Commission, said there was "no justification" for the United States to impose tariffs on steel and aluminum on national security grounds. "Invoking national security would be even more far-fetched in the case of the car industry," he said.

In an interview Thursday on CNBC, Commerce Secretary Wilbur Ross, who is leading the investigation, said the administration was defining national security "broadly," to include the impact on employment and other factors. "Economic security is military security," he said. "And without economic security, you can't have military security."

Mr. Trump has framed the threat of tariffs as a potential source of leverage in talks to rewrite the North American Free Trade Agreement, which have largely stalled over rules governing how carmakers can qualify for Nafta's zero tariffs.

On Wednesday, President Trump said automakers would be "very happy" with his announcement. But few seemed pleased.

While many companies said they were still waiting to see the likely effect of the measure, carmakers, auto parts suppliers and car dealers said it threatened to raise their costs, depress auto sales and jobs in the United States, and make American-made products less competitive worldwide. The industry has already been hit by the tariffs on steel and aluminum, which have weighed on their profit margins, and the threat of looming trade action against China, as well as potential Chinese retaliation.

"If the tariffs actually went into effect, it would upend the supplier industry," said Ann Wilson, senior vice president for government affairs at Motor & Equipment Manufacturers Association, which represents auto parts makers. "We are very dependent on the ability to bring in parts from other parts of the world for final production in the U.S., and if that's no longer financially viable, the question becomes, is the production of vehicles in this country going to be financially viable?"

Kristin Dziczek, the vice president of Industry, Labor & Economics at the Center for Automotive Research, said automakers would be slow to adjust their own investment decisions until they see how any potential tariff decisions might come to pass.

"This is an industry that is big and slow and costs lots of money to build up capacity," she said. "It's unclear how this all proceeds. But what it does immediately is introduce a lot more risk and uncertainty into an industry that doesn't deal well with uncertainty."

Despite the president's vow to defend and strengthen American manufacturing, companies said they worried that the president and his advisers did not understand the complex web of materials and components that are sourced from around the world, and how they support vast numbers of American jobs. They also worried that foreign retaliation could hinder United States automakers from selling abroad.

Mark Zandi, chief economist at Moody's Analytics, estimated that if partners do not retaliate, a 25 percent auto tariff would boost the size of the United States economy by 0.04 percent a year, adding 23,000 jobs in the process. Americans would buy 160,000 fewer vehicles in that time, he estimated, but domestic automobile production would increase by 300,000 vehicles because more of the cars purchased would be made in the United States.

But if other countries were to retaliate with tariffs of their own, Mr. Zandi said, "G.D.P. and jobs will decline."

Several leading Democrats and Republicans criticized Mr. Trump's fondness for injecting confusion into trade matters.

Mr. Trump's strategy "starts with bluster and it tends to end with uncertainty," said Representative Richard E. Neal of Massachusetts, the top Democrat on the Ways and Means Committee. "There's one arena in which measured responses are important, it's in the international trade arena. It's certainly going to have effects on investors and consumers."

Senator Orrin G. Hatch of Utah, the Republican chairman of the finance committee, called the talk of auto tariffs "deeply misguided."

"Taxing cars, trucks and auto parts coming into the country would directly hit American families who need a dependable vehicle," he said.

Senator Michael Bennet, Democrat of Colorado, who has criticized Mr. Trump for exposing farmers and ranchers to retaliation from trading partners, said the president was "trading away our long-term interests in exchange for short-term headlines."

"I don't think there's any coherence to either the trade policies that he's pursuing or how he engages our trading partners in the work of negotiating the agreement," he said.

# White House to Impose Metal Tariffs on E.U., Canada and Mexico

BY ANA SWANSON | MAY 31, 2018

WASHINGTON — The Trump administration said on Thursday that it would impose steep tariffs on metals imported from its closest allies, provoking retaliation against American businesses and consumers and further straining diplomatic ties tested by the president's combative approach.

The European Union, Canada and Mexico, which will face 25 percent tariffs on steel and 10 percent on aluminum, quickly denounced the action and drew up lists of tit-for-tat measures, many aimed at parts of the United States where President Trump enjoys his strongest political support.

The move follows months of uncertainty as the Trump administration dangled potential exemptions for allies in return for concessions on other fronts. In moving forward with tariffs on national security grounds, the administration now faces a crucial test of whether its aggressive strategy will extract promises from trading partners or end up backfiring on the United States economy.

The tariffs "have already had major, positive effects on steel and aluminum workers and jobs and will continue to do so long into the future," White House officials said in a statement. "At the same time, the Trump administration's actions underscore its commitment to good-faith negotiations with our allies to enhance our national security while supporting American workers."

By keeping trading partners guessing, the president has sought to create leverage in trade negotiations, including in talks over the North American Free Trade Agreement with Mexico and Canada. But in the process, he has sowed an atmosphere of chaos among allies as well as manufacturers uncertain about the ultimate impact on their vast supply chains.

The latest twist in the trade drama does little to alleviate the confusion among business owners and foreign leaders. Although the Trump administration signaled a tougher stance with the tariffs, it also left open the possibility for continued negotiations with affected countries.

As trade tensions escalate, Europe, Canada and Mexico are threatening to respond in kind, raising the potential of an all-out trade war.

Chancellor Angela Merkel of Germany, on Thursday, called the tariffs "illegal," while saying "the measures carry the threat of a spiral of escalation that will result in damaging everyone." Prime Minister Justin Trudeau of Canada said it was "inconceivable" that Canada "could be considered a national security threat." Within minutes of the American action, Mexico had detailed a list of goods to target for retaliation, including steel, pork, apples, cranberries and cheeses.

"For the first time in generations, we've really thrown out the rule book with our best trading partners," said Rufus Yerxa, the president of the National Foreign Trade Council, which represents some of the largest exporters in the United States. "We can't expect them to continue business as usual with us if we are throwing out the rules. So that means everything from airplanes to agriculture is on the chopping block."

When the broad tariffs on steel and aluminum were first imposed in March, Mr. Trump quickly carved out temporary exemptions for Canada and Mexico. Later, he added the European Union and other countries with the expectation that they would hash out separate agreements on quotas or similar restrictions. Since then, the Trump administration reached deals with South Korea, Brazil, Australia and Argentina, which agreed to restrain their metals shipments.

But the tariffs loomed in the backdrop as the administration continued to negotiate with Mexico and Canada over Nafta and European officials over other trade matters. Neither talks achieved much.

On Nafta, the Trump administration had been pushing for a quick conclusion to ensure the deal passed through Congress this year. But negotiations have sputtered as the countries remain deeply divided on several important issues, like the rules for automobile manufacturing.

Mr. Trudeau said the countries had the broad lines of "a decent win-win-win deal" last week. He spoke to Mr. Trump and offered to travel to Washington so they could work out the final details.

But Vice President Mike Pence on Tuesday phoned to tell the Canadian prime minister that the precondition of a deal was a sunset clause, meaning the pact would automatically expire unless the three countries voted to continue it. The idea has drawn ire from both foreign leaders and business executives, who say it undercuts the surety that trade agreements are meant to create.

"I had to highlight that there was no possibility of any Canadian prime minister signing a Nafta deal that included a five-year sunset clause," said Mr. Trudeau, "and obviously the visit didn't happen."

European officials had tried offering the United States a limited trade deal. They wanted to avoid tit-for-tat actions — something they view as unproductive, economically perilous and detrimental to the increasingly fraught relationship between the longtime allies.

Germany, in particular, had pressed for a negotiated solution, but officials there grew wary after Mr. Trump announced that he would begin a separate trade investigation into automotive imports. If car tariffs go into effect, they would especially hurt Germany's economy.

Allies have vowed to challenge the legal statute the Trump administration used to roll out the tariffs, which is related to national security.

The Trump administration has argued that imports have weakened the country's industrial base, and, by extension, its ability to produce tanks, weapons and armored vehicles. "We take the view that without a strong economy, you can't have strong national security," the commerce secretary, Wilbur Ross, said Thursday.

The European Union and Canada have objected strongly to the idea that they pose any kind of threat to national security, citing their close alliances and defense agreements with the United States. Jean-Claude Juncker, the president of the European Commission, called the steel and aluminum tariffs announced by the White House on Thursday "protectionism, pure and simple."

With the tariffs set to go into effect at midnight, all three allies are readying their counterattacks.

Canada announced corresponding tariffs on a broad list of American exports, including steel and aluminum, as well as dozens of basic consumer products like ketchup, insecticides and laundry machines. The Canadian tariffs, which go into effect July 1, will cover $12.8 billion worth of American goods, the value of Canadian steel and aluminum exports to the United States in 2017.

"This is the strongest trade action Canada has taken in the post-war era," said Canada's foreign minister, Chrystia Freeland. "This is a very strong Canadian action in response to a very bad U.S. decision."

Along with fighting the tariffs at the World Trade Organization, European officials have been preparing levies on an estimated $3 billion of imported American products in late June. In a joint statement, ministers from France and Germany said the countries would coordinate their response.

"Global trade is not a gunfight at the O.K. Corral," Bruno Le Maire, France's finance minister, said on Thursday after meeting with Mr. Ross. "It's not about who attacks whom, and then wait and see who is still standing at the end."

Whether American consumers and companies get caught in the crossfire depends on how it all plays out.

After the tariffs took effect on China, Russia, Japan and Turkey in late March, prices on steel and aluminum broadly began to rise.

American metal manufacturers say that has helped to level the playing field. Century Aluminum, which has supported the tariffs, said the action "protects thousands of American aluminum workers and puts U.S. national security first."

But it has left businesses that rely on imported metals, like beer makers, auto manufacturers and others, exposed. And now that the tariffs will hit America's closest allies, some early supporters are changing their view.

Canada is the largest supplier of both steel and aluminum to the United States, and the supply chains for many products snake back and forth across the border. The United Steelworkers union, which represents members in Canada as well as the United States, said the decision called "into serious question" the design and direction of the administration's trade strategy.

"The regular chaos surrounding our flawed trade policies is undermining the ability to project a reasoned course and ensure that we can improve domestic production and employment," the union said in a statement.

The Aluminum Association, the industry trade group, also said it was disappointed. Heidi Brock, the group's president, said the tariffs would do little to address the larger issue of overcapacity in China "while potentially alienating allies and disrupting supply chains that more than 97 percent of U.S. aluminum industry jobs rely upon."

The steel and aluminum tariffs already appear to be hurting construction companies, retailers and manufacturers — by raising their costs and injecting uncertainty into the price and availability of the metals going forward.

The Federal Reserve's latest Beige Book, a collection of anecdotes about the health of regional economies, contains more than two dozen references to business fears that the administration's trade policies, and the steel and aluminum tariffs in particular, would hurt sales and profits.

"These tariffs are hitting the wrong target," said Representative Kevin Brady, Republican of Texas. "When it comes to unfairly traded steel and aluminum, Mexico, Canada and Europe are not the problem — China is."

In a more pointed statement, Senator Ben Sasse, Republican of Nebraska, called the tariffs "dumb."

"Europe, Canada and Mexico are not China, and you don't treat allies the same way you treat opponents," he said.

# After Taunting Mexico, Trump Takes Action With Tariffs. But Do Mexicans Still Care?

BY ELISABETH MALKIN AND PAULINA VILLEGAS  |  JUNE 1, 2018

MEXICO CITY — For more than two years, Donald J. Trump has attacked Mexico to excite his political base, threatening walls, mass deportations and an end to a nearly 25-year free trade deal between Mexico and the United States.

As frequent targets of Mr. Trump's ire, many Mexicans have learned to take it in stride, finding that the bark is often worse than the bite.

On Thursday, however, the Trump administration clamped down on Mexico's steel industry, along with those of Europe and Canada, imposing a 25 percent tariff on Mexican steel imports — the first real attack on the $1.5 billion in trade that crosses the border both ways every day.

Almost immediately, Mexico responded with a round of counter-tariffs, retaliations aimed straight at the heart of Mr. Trump's base of political support. The reprisal had been drawn up for some time, in anticipation of the tariffs, which were first announced in March and delayed until now.

Yet there was no hand-wringing by Mexico, no public uproar or Twitter storm. Just a series of countermeasures, explained in a measured release.

Mexico's response, in some ways, is a reflection of just how accustomed the nation has grown to the actions taken by Mr. Trump. Its position regarding cooperation with the United States — on trade, migration or security — "will not vary, neither because of offensive rhetoric, nor because of unilateral and unjustified measures of this kind," said Foreign Minister Luis Videgaray.

Mexico has adopted a poised and consistent stance in its responses, one it has refined over the course of the two years that Mr. Trump has lashed out at the country with insults and threats, first as a candidate, then as president-elect and now as president.

To many analysts, Mexico has learned to soldier past the taunts.

"It is not that we don't care, it is just that Mexicans have internalized it," said Carlos Heredia, a professor at CIDE, a Mexico City university. "It no longer carries the element of surprise. We have been dealing with it and hearing it for two years, so it has already had its effect."

Mexico has said repeatedly that the issue of steel tariffs will not define the negotiations over Nafta. And, more broadly, Mexican officials have also said they will not sign anything that is not in their country's national interest.

That Mr. Trump imposed the tariffs on Mexico as part of a global strategy also takes much of the sting out.

To many here, the steel tariffs are simply a stronger attempt — moving from words to action — to forcefully impose his worldview on the bilateral relationship. Rather than abide by current agreements, or understandings, the United States government has been subsumed by the compulsive, often personal agenda of the president, analysts said.

"What Trump is doing is imposing his vision of the world," said Carlos Elizondo, a professor at the School of Government at the Monterrey Institute of Technology and Higher Education. "The Mexican government is not letting this pass, but rather putting out the message that we are playing by the rules and that we are all in the same game."

There are two potential implications for Mexico: One is electoral, the other commercial.

Mexico is gearing up for one of the most consequential presidential elections in more than a decade, with the voting set for July 1. But so far, Mr. Trump's actions have done surprisingly little to move the needle.

The candidates largely backed the Mexican government retaliation on Thursday, and more generally they speak with the same voice when it comes to not allowing Mr. Trump to bully Mexico.

It has been that way through much of the election cycle here, where domestic issues have dominated the discourse, and Mr. Trump's potshots have long since become background noise for voters.

On the commercial side, however, the implications could be greater. While Mexico responded forcefully, and immediately, any further escalation would certainly carry a price with it — for both countries.

Along with tariffs on flat steel imports from the United States, Mexico will impose tariffs on lamps, pork legs and shoulders, sausages and prepared foods, apples, grapes, cranberries, various cheeses and other products.

The products were selected to affect exporters in states that are politically important to Mr. Trump. American agricultural exporters have been particularly concerned that Mexico would retaliate against their products.

Mr. Trump's move could also disrupt the steel market in the region, experts warned, forcing Mexico to look to other trading partners for their supplies. Despite Mr. Trump's obsession with reversing trade deficits, the country that runs a deficit in steel is Mexico, not the United States.

According to Mexico's steel industry association, the United States sold $3.6 billion more to Mexico over the past two years than Mexico sold to the United States.

Experts said that tariffs would have an impact on some Mexican steel producers who export specific products to the United States, but that the larger effect might be on the companies in Mexico that import American steel for use in the auto industry.

The decision by the Trump administration was explained as a national security measure, a move that summoned sharp rebukes from all nations affected, including Mexico. The administration also

President Trump has frequently threatened to end a nearly 25-year free trade deal between Mexico and the United States.

said it was conducting a similar investigation into imported cars — a market where the Mexican economy is deeply intertwined with the United States.

For renegotiations on the North American Free Trade Agreement, some experts think that the move on Thursday could heighten tensions between the nations during already tense talks. Now that the United States has taken concrete action, the stakes are higher, potentially leading Mexico and Canada to dig in their heels more in the face of American demands.

"Trump had delayed the tariffs on Mexico and Canada pending results from the negotiations, and threatening to impose them to pressure more," said Jeffrey A. Weldon, director of the political science program at the Mexico Autonomous Institute of Technology. "Trump may have seen the end of the line."

The tariffs are also unlikely to force the Mexican government's hand, especially given current electoral dynamics. The candidate of the governing party, José Antonio Meade, is a distant third in polls and is unlikely to win. That means there is little pressure to sign a deal quickly simply to help his campaign.

In the short term, analysts expected that the trade battle now underway would quickly result in price increases on certain products on supermarket shelves in Mexico as the retaliatory tariffs take effect.

A greater, enduring fear, according to Enrique Dussel Peters, an economist at the National Autonomous University of Mexico, is that Mr. Trump will suddenly pull the United States from Nafta, as he has threatened.

Mr. Weldon said he has been expecting it. "Others say, 'No one can be that dumb,' " he said. "My response has always been: Don't bet against his base."

"That would be a much more serious thing," he said, "and that would directly hit Mexico."

# Chinese Tariffs Are Already Hitting Trump Voters

EDITORIAL | BY THE NEW YORK TIMES | JUNE 15, 2018

IN IOWA, where farmers raise 40 to 50 million pigs annually, President Trump's tariffs on steel and aluminum from Mexico have already cost producers $560 million, according to an Iowa State University economist. How can that be, you ask. Mexico has threatened countervailing tariffs that include a 20 percent tariff on American pork. That prospect alone sent hog prices tumbling. If you like barbecued ribs, this could be a great summer for you. If you raise the pigs, you may be eating more barbecued beans.

Soybean growers throughout the Midwest are nervously watching as China, which buys a quarter of American soybeans, takes aim at their crop in response to the Trump administration's announcement that it will move ahead with $50 billion in tariffs on "industrially significant technologies" in more than 1,000 categories. Trade between the two countries has been "very unfair, for a very long time," the American president said in a statement. Mr. Trump vowed that he would add to that list if China retaliated — which is what most countries do in this situation. Indeed, the Chinese Ministry of Commerce has said to expect as much. Oh great, Middle America collectively sighs.

Local newspapers across the heartland are full of similar tales of value destruction and lost income as a result of Trump trade war tweetism. In Great Lakes states, traditional steel makers might benefit from the administration's 25 percent tariff on foreign steel. But for steel users, it's an entirely different story. Shortly after tariffs were announced, steel suppliers, no longer as fearful of price competition, began jacking up prices — they're no fools. That has meant a 40 percent increase since January in the cost of steel for their customers who use it in their finished products, according to the U.S.

Chamber of Commerce. They can either pass that increase on to you or be less profitable.

The story is the same with aluminum: Brewers are forecasting that they'll pay $347.7 million more for aluminum cans. That has small craft-beer makers such as Melvin Brewing in Alpine, Wyo., which packages 75 percent of its products in cans, fretting about impending prices rises and the risks of passing them along to consumers. Try not to be bitter about it.

Mr. Trump's obsession with Canada is particularly strange, and his outburst directed at Prime Minister Justin Trudeau ("Very dishonest & weak.") is particularly petulant. When you tote up the goods and services traded between the two nations in 2017, the United States counted a $8.4 billion surplus. Canada buys more American agricultural exports than any other nation, $24 billion worth. The Canadians sent $7 billion worth of steel here last year while we sold a similar amount to them.

In the dairy industry, Canada supports its farmers with regulations that restrict the milk supply but gives direct subsidies. In the United States, dairy farmers are truly suffering. Prices are below production costs in part because farmers continued to overbuild their herds despite lagging demand. Yet Mr. Trump is essentially blaming Canada for our failed agriculture policy.

These are not small or isolated examples, as Commerce Secretary Wilbur Ross seems to believe. The losses are real now and could become enormous in the future. Job losses from the metal tariffs alone could top 400,000, according to an analysis by Trade Partnership Worldwide, a nonpartisan consultancy that supports free trade. So while U.S. Steel can celebrate the restart of two blast furnaces in Granite City, Ill., and bring back about 800 workers, 7,500 jobs will be lost elsewhere, the consultancy estimates.

None of this reality seems to have registered with the president, who is obsessed with the trade deficit. "Why should I, as president of the United States, allow countries to continue to make massive trade surpluses, as they have for decades, while our farmers, workers & tax-payers have such a big and unfair price to pay?" Mr. Trump tweeted.

As any number of Nobel economists have tried to explain, a trade deficit by itself is neither good nor bad. American citizens benefit from being able to buy competitively priced Mexican produce, Japanese cars and Canadian steel. And foreign countries use the earnings from those sales to invest in American stocks, bonds and industries. Our currency stays strong without our making our export products too expensive. Japan ran trade surpluses for 30 consecutive years until 2011, but that did not prevent its economy from sputtering.

And as for protecting American workers, with a 3.8 percent unemployment rate, the number of job openings now exceeds the number of people who are unemployed, according to The Wall Street Journal.

Republican lawmakers, long proponents of free trade, portray themselves as impotent to halt the president's trade warmongering. The Senate majority leader, Mitch McConnell of Kentucky, has said there's not much he can do, even as the European Union has put his state's thriving bourbon industry in the cross hairs with a proposed 25 percent tariff. Kentucky and Tennessee sell $1 billion worth of liquor to foreign countries. In Wisconsin, home state of House Speaker Paul Ryan, companies that make fishing boats and motorcycles (Harley-Davidson) are also being targeted. So are cranberry growers. Senator Bob Corker, Republican of Tennessee, got nowhere when he proposed legislation requiring congressional approval of tariffs that are imposed in the name of national security, as the recent ones were.

Trade deals can be renegotiated — sure, let's get a better deal with China — as countries and their economies evolve and the needs of their citizens change. The American economy was once dependent on manufacturing; today, service exports carry much more of the load. It doesn't mean we don't build jets or cars or chips, but it does mean that the software and computing algorithms that operate in those things may have as much value as the hardware and may provide better jobs.

Collectively, they account for about a sixth of global trade.

The agreement will "serve as a foundation for building a broader free-trade area" across Asia, Taro Kono, Japan's foreign minister, said in a statement.

Pointedly, the potential members of what is now called the Comprehensive and Progressive Agreement for Trans-Pacific Partnership came to an early agreement on the broad outline of a deal while many of their leaders were meeting with Mr. Trump in Vietnam — itself a potential member of the new trading group.

Some details of a new deal, including when rules would be phased in, still need to be determined, and prospective member states like Canada raised last-minute concerns. But a new deal could be announced as soon as early next year.

Other countries are slowly but surely making progress on their own sweeping trade deals, without any participation from the United States. China is negotiating a potential deal with 16 Asia-Pacific countries, including Japan, India and South Korea. The European Union and Japan hope to strike separate trade pacts with a group of South American countries, Brazil and Argentina among them.

From tough talk on China ("they took our jobs") to casting doubt on the decades-old North American Free Trade Agreement ("the worst trade deal ever made"), Mr. Trump has threatened to lob a grenade at an increasingly integrated global economic system.

His administration has questioned years of efforts to lower global trade barriers, arguing that they hurt American workers and led to big trade deficits. It also means dealing with nations one-on-one, rejecting the regional and global pacts his predecessors pursued.

But other factors are pushing the rest of the world to fill the void left by the United States. China's rise as a regional and economic power is driving other nations either to join with it or to join together to counter it. Fast development in places like Southeast Asia means potential new markets for all kinds of products. The absence of the United States means potential opportunities for others.

"At some point, the administration may begin to see that this was a strategic mistake and that dropping out of trade is not in the interest of American workers," said Rufus Yerxa, president of the National Foreign Trade Council, a lobbying group that represents companies like Walmart, Ford and Microsoft.

"We've got to compete and be a winner in global markets — and the danger is, the strategy is divisive," he added.

More worrying for some is the possibility that the Trump administration is ceding its position as global leader to China, a rising economic and political influence in the region.

"The U.S. has lost its leadership role," said Jayant Menon, an economist at the Asian Development Bank. "And China is quickly replacing it."

Under the new Trans-Pacific trade deal, members would enjoy tariff-free trade with one another. That would allow companies in the member countries to have faster and better access to other markets than their American rivals.

But there are still challenges ahead of the group, and not all the prospective member states meeting in Danang, Vietnam, were in complete accord over the finer details of a new deal.

"We are pleased that progress is being made towards a possible agreement, but there is still some work to be done," François-Philippe Champagne, Canada's minister of international trade, said in a statement. He added that Canada would sign a deal only once its interests had been addressed.

Even without the United States, the deal would be the largest trade agreement in history. It is intended to increase protections for intellectual property in some countries, while opening more markets to free trade in agricultural products and digital services around the region. It also has provisions on improving working conditions, although there is debate about the likely results.

In a statement posted online, the Australian government said that the agreement in principle demonstrated the 11 countries' "commitment to open markets, to combat protectionism and to advance regional economic integration."

The 11 countries working toward the new agreement are Japan, Australia, Canada, Mexico, Singapore, Malaysia, Vietnam, Chile, Peru, New Zealand and Brunei.

Mr. Trump has expressed support for the nation's regional allies even as he rejects or criticizes trade deals with them. He reiterated American support for cooperation on security during his stops in Japan and South Korea.

In China, he went out of his way to woo President Xi Jinping, going so far as to suggest that the trade deficit with the United States was the fault of past American administrations rather than of China itself.

"I don't blame China," Mr. Trump said in a tweet on Friday morning shortly before leaving for Vietnam.

"The U.S. has been the driving force, not just behind the global economic order, but also pursuing higher standards on free trade and securing provisions that go way above the World Trade Organization obligations," said Stephen Olson, a former United States trade negotiator who worked on Nafta. "If the U.S. abdicates that role, it puts us in uncharted territory," he added.

In the absence of American leadership, Japan has driven the new round of talks. Prime Minister Shinzo Abe has spoken of the countries working on an agreement as Ocean's Eleven, after the movie.

Japan's long-term hope is that the United States will eventually return to the fold.

"We will just go ahead and make it and we will welcome the United States back if they decide to do so," said Ichiro Fujisaki, a former Japanese ambassador to Washington. Completing a deal now, he said, "makes the possibility of the U.S. coming back more likely."

The new agreement has been crafted with the hope that the United States will one day participate. Some of the provisions — among them ones that the United States lobbied for — could ultimately be suspended, including some on copyright protection.

Given the intensity with which Mr. Trump excoriated the original deal, it seems unlikely that this administration will come back to the table.

"It will be difficult for the administration to backtrack," said Wendy Cutler, a former United States trade negotiator who worked on the Trans-Pacific deal and is now managing director of the Washington office of the Asia Society Policy Institute.

But other countries like Korea, the Philippines and Thailand are expected to join once the deal is ratified, said Ms. Cutler.

For members, the pact could offer a sense of security in a time when a number of politicians around the world are questioning the impact of trade and globalization.

Speaking last week, Prime Minister Malcolm Turnbull of Australia said the deal promised "greater transparency and a stronger rule of law, in a world which is dangerously short of both," referring to the "siren songs of populists, advocating protectionism."

"The T.P.P. creates rules of the road to match the new economic world we are living in," Mr. Turnbull said.

Notably, the Trans-Pacific pact includes Mexico and Canada, which are at loggerheads with the Trump administration over Nafta. Mr. Trump has raised the prospect of the demise of that agreement, citing the movement of industrial jobs from the United States to those countries.

"There is a genuine risk that the U.S. is going to further disengage from regional economic interaction," said Christopher Nelson, editor of the Nelson Report, a foreign policy and trade newsletter. "And from the corporate standpoint, American companies are disadvantaged competitively if we're not out there with both feet playing the game."

# Trump Trade Measures Set Off a Global Legal Pushback

BY ANA SWANSON | FEB. 9, 2018

WASHINGTON — Tariffs imposed by the United States late last month are prompting a wave of litigation from other nations, including Canada and China, escalating concerns that the Trump administration's more aggressive trade stance could worsen international relations and spur retaliatory actions on American goods sent abroad.

On Wednesday, three Canadian solar companies filed a lawsuit in a New York court over tariffs on solar cells and panels that the United States imposed in late January, claiming these penalties violate American law and the terms of the North American Free Trade Agreement. That same day, the European Union became the fourth member of the World Trade Organization to request discussions with the United States for compensation for the solar tariffs, following similar requests by China, Taiwan and South Korea.

Chinese officials also confirmed last weekend that they had launched a separate investigation into whether American exports of sorghum were receiving government subsidies or being sold at unfairly low prices abroad — a measure widely interpreted as a response to the Trump administration's ratcheting up of trade barriers.

With the Trump administration considering further trade actions on Chinese products and foreign metals this year, some trade analysts are concerned that other American products, from soybeans to Kentucky bourbon, could become a target for retaliation.

Darci Vetter, a former chief agricultural negotiator for the United States trade representative, called China's sorghum case just the latest example of American agriculture landing in the cross hairs as trade tensions rise.

"Unfortunately, the agriculture sector knows from experience that when tit-for-tat trade actions begin, agricultural products are the first to be hit," Ms. Vetter said. "Given the size and importance of China's market for a variety of U.S. ag products, we are concerned it won't be the last."

The Trump administration announced Jan. 22 that it would impose tariffs of up to 50 percent on imported washing machines and 30 percent on imported solar cells and modules, responding to a pair of trade cases alleging that cheap foreign products were degrading American manufacturing capacity.

Those tariffs were not as high as what the companies bringing the complaints had requested, or some of the recommendations made by the officials of the United States International Trade Commission. Still, many economists, consumer groups and businesses warned that the tariffs would lead to higher prices and could even end up costing more jobs than they would save.

These groups are still waiting to see whether the Trump administration fulfills its most ambitious plans for remaking trade policy. In the coming months, the administration is expected to introduce a hefty penalty on China for encroaching on American intellectual property, which could include tariffs on consumer electronics or restrictions on Chinese investment in the United States.

The fate of two separate trade actions, on imports of steel and aluminum, appears less certain.

Last June, President Trump said that the steel industry would be seeing action "very soon." But the idea of these tariffs was met with a swift backlash from industries that use the metals to produce other goods, like carmakers, as well as some Defense Department officials.

Since the Commerce Department submitted its reports on the investigations to the president last month, the cases have not been mentioned in official statements, including the White House's summary of its current trade actions released after the president's State of the Union address.

The resignation this week of Rob Porter, the White House staff secretary, who was responsible for organizing weekly meetings of

White House trade advisers and bridging deep divides in views on trade among the staff, throws the fate of these measures into further question.

Depending on what happens at the World Trade Organization, the United States could see further retaliation against the solar tariff, said Allan T. Marks, a lawyer at Milbank, Tweed, Hadley and McCloy.

The World Trade Organization will now consider whether countries like China had sufficient opportunity to consult with the United States before the tariffs were imposed, and if the United States followed its rules for creating such temporary safeguards for its industries.

Mr. Marks declined to speculate on the potential results, but said that the most recent precedent could be troubling for the United States. The last time that the United States imposed these kinds of tariffs, on steel imports under President George W. Bush in 2002, the World Trade Organization ruled that they were illegal, clearing the way for countries to lawfully retaliate against the United States. Under the threat of retaliation, the Bush administration withdrew the steel tariffs in 2003.

"You could see retaliation from exporting countries like China that are hurt by the safeguard action," Mr. Marks said. "And we'll probably get there. That's what happened for steel."

# Trump Trade Sanctions Aimed at China Could Ensnare Canada

BY ANA SWANSON | FEB. 25, 2018

WASHINGTON — China is the main target of possible tough new United States trade measures against low-priced imports of steel and aluminum. But the sanctions threaten to ensnare America's closest allies, particularly Canada.

Earlier this month, the Commerce Department declared the steel and aluminum imports a national security threat, and President Trump must decide by mid-April whether to impose sanctions, including quotas and tariffs.

But all of the options presented by the Commerce Department would affect Canada, a longtime supplier of metals to the American military and industry. Imports from Britain, Australia, South Korea and other countries could also be hit.

President Trump could choose to accept one of the Commerce Department's recommendations or fashion his own remedy. Either way, the issue highlights the difficulty the Trump administration faces as it seeks to limit imports in a world where companies routinely make, ship and sell products across borders.

The potential trade action is further straining already-tense relations between the United States and Canada, two of the world's most integrated economies. The countries have clashed over the North American Free Trade Agreement, American tariffs on Canadian lumber, and Canada's recent complaint to the World Trade Organization about American trade practices.

Last Thursday, James Mattis, the Defense Secretary, published a public letter concluding that the decline of the American industry as a result of unfair trade posed a threat to national security, a position aligned with the Commerce Department's. But he urged the administration to proceed cautiously, particularly with regard to allies.

The Defense Department "continues to be concerned about the negative impact on our key allies regarding the recommended options within the reports," Mr. Mattis wrote. He urged the administration to consider tariffs targeted at specific countries and to focus on what he described as the underlying problem — Chinese overproduction.

Yet the United States could face a challenge in crafting trade sanctions that circumvent allies and target China. It has already imposed a variety of restrictions on Chinese aluminum and steel. But American steel and aluminum producers argue that China still harms them indirectly by routing goods through third countries, as well as depressing global prices to a level where American manufacturers cannot compete.

Although China has promised to cut its steel and aluminum capacity, it has made only slow, modest progress. That is why some American metal makers have argued for broader protections.

Canada accounted for more than half of American imports of aluminum in 2016, followed distantly by Russia and the United Arab Emirates. Canada also made up the largest share of American steel imports in 2016 — 17 percent — followed by Brazil, South Korea, Mexico and Turkey. China did not rank among the top 10 suppliers of either metal.

"From a defense perspective, it makes no sense to limit imports from Canada in the future," said Alf Barrios, the chief executive of Rio Tinto Aluminum, which exports aluminum from Canada to the United States. "Canada is a longstanding, reliable supply for any needs the United States might have."

Canada's inclusion in the Commerce Department recommendations was unexpected, in part because companies and workers have been relatively united in calling for the country to be exempted. The operations of many metal makers — as well as the United Steelworkers, their largest union — stretch across the border. Under law, Canada is included as part of the United States defense industrial base, and the growth of its aluminum industry dates back to supporting the United States during World War II.

Kathleen Wynne, the premier of Ontario, said the recent level of animosity and trade tensions with the United States had surprised Canadians. "We see ourselves as close friends," she said. "It's unexpected that we would stand to be damaged by the United States, and vice versa."

Ken Neumann, the national director of United Steelworkers, struck a similar note. "There is no justification to include Canada with countries that systematically violate trade laws and engage in the dumping of illegally subsidized aluminum and steel," he said after the release of the Commerce Department report.

Canada is one of several allies that could be affected. Britain, Australia, Europe and Japan would also be included under the kind of blanket tariff or quota recently floated by the Commerce Department.

The measures could fall particularly hard on South Korea, which was named as one of the countries that would face a 53 percent tariff on its steel exports, along with China, Brazil, India, Russia, Turkey and six others, under one potential scenario in the report.

The United States has been seeking South Korea's cooperation to combat a nuclear threat from North Korea. But the Trump administration has simultaneously pursued the country on trade, largely because South Korea maintains a large trade surplus with the United States. The administration is renegotiating its free trade deal with South Korea, and the country was a target of an earlier tariff on washing machines.

Including countries like Canada could lead to unintended ramifications for the United States military and economy.

Many products made in America use foreign metals, including the Ford F-150, a classic American truck that is consistently ranked as one of the most "made-in-America" vehicles in an industry known for sourcing parts from around the world.

The truck's engine and transmission are American-made, and the truck is assembled in plants in Dearborn, Mich., and Claycomo, Mo. Even so, the truck is made of Canadian aluminum, some of which comes from Rio Tinto's aluminum works in Quebec — an area with plentiful hydropower, which is needed for the energy-intensive process of producing aluminum.

From Quebec, some aluminum travels to a plant in upstate New York owned by Novelis, which combines it with recycled aluminum and rolls it out into wide sheets for Ford.

Another 15 percent of the value of the truck's components come from Mexico. Its window wipers come from a factory in Matamoros, some of its wheels from Chihuahua, and some of the pistons in its engine from Ramos Arizpe.

The auto industry says this web of North American suppliers allows it to produce cars and trucks at a quality and a price to compete with products made around the world. Ford exports the truck back to Canada, and last year it announced that it would begin exporting vehicles to China as well.

Economists say the companies that make aluminum into car bodies and soda cans employ far more people than the smelters that make raw aluminum itself. Novelis, which specializes in recycling and rolling aluminum out into sheets, announced in January that it would invest $300 million to open a new factory in Guthrie, Ky., to make the aluminum sheeting used in cars.

The same trends are true in the steel industry. In mid-February, 15 American industry associations that buy steel to make their products wrote a letter to Mr. Trump arguing that, by raising the price of steel, restrictions on imports could do more harm than good. They said they represented more than one million jobs in the United States, compared with about 80,000 jobs in primary steel production.

Other economic forces are driving aluminum smelting from the United States. Aluminum manufacturing is extremely energy intensive, so it has tended to go to parts of the world with cheap excess energy, like the Middle East, Iceland and Canada. Smelters in the United States must compete with other, more profitable businesses for electricity, like computer server farms.

# Trump's Tariffs Prompt Global Threats of Retaliation

BY ANA SWANSON | MARCH 2, 2018

WASHINGTON — A day after President Trump took a swing at United States trading partners by threatening stiff and sweeping tariffs on steel and aluminum, they hit back. They promised to retaliate against quintessential American goods like Kentucky bourbon, bluejeans and Harley-Davidson motorcycles.

That is likely to turn into a wave of protest aimed at American products as other countries, including traditional allies, respond to Mr. Trump's plan to clamp down on imports of metals from overseas.

Canada, China and the European Union have already said they would respond with tariffs of their own that could lead to billions of

LUKE SHARRETT FOR THE NEW YORK TIMES

An employee moves empty bourbon barrels manufactured by the Independent Stave Company in Frankfort, Ky. It is just one American product that could be the target of retaliatory tariffs from important trading partners.

dollars in American export losses. Those levies would harm the farmers and business interests that the Trump administration has promised to protect and would fuel a trade fight that could undermine the president's goal of strengthening American industry.

Li Xinchuang, the vice chairman of the China Iron and Steel Association, called the president's move "stupid," saying, "Trump's decision does no good to everyone except a few American steel enterprises."

And John M. Weekes, Canada's negotiator for the North American Free Trade Agreement in the early 1990s, said the president's "notion is going down very badly in Canada."

"It certainly will have a negative effect on our bilateral relationship," he said.

American businesses are more tied to the global economy than ever before, and the Trump administration is seeking concessions from trading partners to put American companies on a more competitive footing. Negotiators from Canada, Mexico and the United States were meeting in Mexico City to hash out changes to Nafta, and Washington is trying to revise a trade deal with South Korea. The possibility of tariffs complicates both efforts.

Mr. Trump appeared unmoved by the blowback, posting a series of Twitter messages on Friday defending his proposal to impose tariffs of 25 percent on steel and 10 percent on aluminum.

"We must protect our country and our workers. Our steel industry is in bad shape. IF YOU DON'T HAVE STEEL, YOU DON'T HAVE A COUNTRY!" Mr. Trump tweeted.

Yet the United States does not control the global economy, and the tariffs, which Mr. Trump is expected to sign next week, could incite other countries to challenge it at the World Trade Organization. If the organization rules against the United States, that will test the Trump administration's willingness to follow global trade rules.

The tariffs rest on a little-used legal provision that allows Mr. Trump to restrict imports to try to bolster the American industrial base in the interest of national security. That power will face scrutiny by the World Trade Organization but, perhaps more significant, could prompt other countries to follow suit in using national security as a reason to wall off their markets.

American technology companies, agricultural producers and other industries could ultimately lose business abroad as nations seek to erect similar barriers.

Robert L. Shanks, Ford Motor's chief financial officer, said commodities markets had already started to price in increases for steel and aluminum on the expectation that Mr. Trump would impose the tariffs. The effect on Ford, he said, is "not positive" given the automaker uses those metals in the cars they produce.

The European Union detailed a three-step plan to penalize $3.5 billion of American trade — the same amount of European steel and aluminum the bloc estimates would be harmed by the planned tariffs. It proposed taxing American exports including bourbon, bluejeans, orange juice, cranberries, rice and motorcycles. The European Union could then take action to protect their own metal makers from a surge in imports, and bring a case against the United States at the World Trade Organization.

A European Union official said that the bloc had been preparing for the announcement for months and that everything was in place for a swift, proportionate response.

The measures were intended to put pressure on politically sensitive areas, trade analysts said. Harley-Davidson motorcycles are made in the home district of Speaker Paul D. Ryan, Republican of Wisconsin. Orange juice comes from the swing state of Florida. Restrictions on Kentucky bourbon could add pressure on the Senate majority leader, Mitch McConnell, who is from the state.

Retaliation could hit hardest in many of the rural communities that were strongholds for Mr. Trump. Farmers are among America's largest exporters, and often become a target in trade spats, said Darci Vetter, the former chief agricultural negotiator for the United

States trade representative. She said the agricultural community was "rightly nervous" about the prospect.

Canada and Mexico were America's No. 1 and No. 3 largest agricultural markets in 2016, and South Korea is a major market for beef, corn, pork and fresh fruit, Ms. Vetter said. The United States exports cotton to Turkey and wheat and dairy to Brazil, other major suppliers of steel.

Senator John Cornyn of Texas expressed concern on Friday that America's trading partners might respond by imposing tariffs on agriculture, which he said would "devastate our agricultural communities."

Other countries have been less specific, but no less emphatic, in their threats. Canada's minister of foreign affairs, Chrystia Freeland, said that Canada stood ready to defend its trade interests, while the Australian trade minister, Steven Ciobo, said the tariffs would set off retaliatory measures that would hurt everyone.

American steel companies are a key constituency for Mr. Trump, who won the support of some blue-collar workers by pledging to revive United States industry. The steel industry has shed hundreds of thousands of jobs in the country in the past two decades, partly because of automation and partly because of a flood of production from China, which has driven down global prices to a level where some American mills cannot compete.

American steel and aluminum companies were the loudest in applauding the president's efforts to help their industries. Labor unions and Rust Belt politicians, including Democrats, commended Mr. Trump for fulfilling an important political promise he made during the campaign.

"Our view is we needed some relief on illegally traded products," said John J. Ferriola, chairman, president and chief executive of Nucor Corporation. "Whatever the remedy, it had to be comprehensive trade relief."

On Fox Business Network Friday morning, Peter Navarro, a top White House trade adviser, said he did not believe any country would retaliate, "for the simple reason that we are the most lucrative and biggest market in the world."

"They know they're cheating us, and all we're doing is standing up for ourselves," he added.

Mr. Trump's announcement on Thursday was a clear signal to many observers that the pro-trade advisers in the Trump administration — who have tried to stay the president's hand on tariffs and withdrawing from trade agreements — might have less influence than they believe. That could further fuel trade tensions and make it less likely that the United States will be able to reach the types of bilateral or multilateral agreements that have helped expand American exports.

Antonio Ortiz-Mena, a senior adviser at the Albright Stonebridge Group, said that if the United States was willing to impose penalties like these on its close trading partners, other countries would be less eager to negotiate trade deals with the United States. "What is the benefit of having a special relationship?" he asked. "I think there could be a lot of unintended and unforeseen consequences."

# E.U. Pledges to Fight Back on Trump Tariffs as Trade War Looms

BY MILAN SCHREUER | MARCH 7, 2018

BRUSSELS — European Union officials unveiled an array of tariffs on Wednesday that they would place on American-made goods if the United States followed through on President Trump's plan to impose penalties on imported steel and aluminum, raising the specter of a trade war.

The announcement in Brussels was the latest rebuke to Mr. Trump's proposed tariffs, which have met with consternation domestically and with threats of retaliation abroad. The president's top economic adviser, Gary D. Cohn, said on Tuesday that he was resigning, a move widely believed to be linked to the trade plan, which he had lobbied against. Republican leaders, including Paul D. Ryan, the House speaker, have also railed against the tariffs.

Internationally, the plan for the new American tariffs — blanket penalties of 25 percent on imported steel and of 10 percent on aluminum — have drawn concern from allies including Britain and Canada, as well as from rivals like China. The European Union had warned of retaliatory charges last week, and outlined those plans on Wednesday.

Such a move by the United States would "put thousands of European jobs in jeopardy, and it has to be met by a firm and proportionate response," Cecilia Malmstrom, the European Union commissioner for trade, said at a news conference in Brussels. European officials have been meeting with their counterparts in Washington, urging them to revisit the plans, she added.

If the American tariffs are put in place, Ms. Malmstrom said, Brussels could take three steps: It could take the case to the World Trade Organization, add safeguards to protect the European Union against steel diverted from the United States, and impose tariffs on a series of American-made goods.

A provisional list of items being targeted ranges from steel to T-shirts, also including bed linen, chewing tobacco, cranberries and orange juice, among other products. The overall size of the business affected is relatively small, worth about 2.8 billion euros, or $3.5 billion, in imports, paling in comparison with the nearly €250 billion of goods the 28-nation bloc bought from the United States in 2016.

European leaders were quick to stress that they did not want to trigger a wider trade dispute, with Donald Tusk, the president of the European Council, saying in a tweet that trade wars were "bad and easy to lose," a reference to an earlier tweet by Mr. Trump in which he claimed they were "good and easy to win."

Officials elsewhere have also tried to cool tensions. Christine Lagarde, the head of the International Monetary Fund, warned in an interview on French radio that in a trade war, "nobody wins, one generally finds losers on both sides."

But it reflects concern in Europe over the possible impact of new American tariffs, notably on steel. The United States is the world's largest importer of steel, and while many of Mr. Trump's arguments have focused on cheap steel from countries like China, the European Union as a whole is the single biggest exporter of steel to the United States. At the same time, the region is concerned that cheap steel that had been destined for the United States could now flood the Continent, putting significant pressure on European producers.

While retaliation from Brussels appears limited for now, it could have an impact on American domestic politics. Bourbon, one of the products that European officials have targeted, is made in Kentucky, the home state of Mitch McConnell, the Senate majority leader. Other items that could face tariffs are motorcycles, and the corporate headquarters of Harley-Davidson are in Wisconsin, Mr. Ryan's state.

"The Europeans have rights, too, to retaliate," said Peter Chase, a former American diplomat who is now a senior fellow at the German Marshall Fund in Brussels focusing on trade. "The E.U. is concerned that behind it all, there are people in the U.S. administration that don't care that there might be damage to the international system of rule of law that we have created."

The list, which was leaked on Monday and has been referred to by the European Commission president, Jean-Claude Juncker, is subject to the agreement of the bloc's 28 member states.

It highlights how sharply the outlook on trade between the United States and Europe has shifted. Since 2013, Washington and Brussels have been negotiating a vast trade deal, known as the Trans-Atlantic Trade and Investment Partnership.

By late 2016, however, those talks appeared to have reached a stalemate, and Mr. Trump's withdrawal from a similar pact with Pacific Rim countries early in his presidency signaled the death of the European agreement, as well.

The strong negative reaction to Mr. Trump's planned tariffs appears to have had little impact on the president, who insisted this week that he would not back down.

On Tuesday, Mr. Trump singled out the European Union, which he said had "not treated us very well, and it's been a very, very unfair trade situation." The president warned that the United States would also consider raising its tariffs on cars made within the bloc if the European Union were to retaliate.

While he left the door open for compromise with allies, tensions are rising in Europe.

"We've loaded the guns," said Charles de Lusignan, a spokesman for the European Steel Association, a lobbying group, "and we're ready to use them in case the aggression comes."

# A Storm of Reaction to Trump's Tariffs

**BY THE NEW YORK TIMES | MARCH 8, 2018**

President Trump's tariffs on steel and aluminum have elicited strong reactions from leaders in government, business and other organizations around the world. Most of them oppose the tariffs, with many leaders saying they fear that the tariffs could escalate a trade war. Below are several notable reactions.

"If you put tariffs against your allies, one wonders who the enemies are."

**MARIO DRAGHI**
President of the European Central Bank

"Choosing a trade war is a mistaken prescription. The outcome will only be harmful. China would have to make a justified and necessary response."

**WANG YI**
China's foreign minister

"The message is that we believe in the value of an open economy and economic integration of countries in order to generate greater prosperity for our people and our nations. I think that is a tremendously important value at a time when certain sectors of the world are sending messages that run contrary to this choice, preaching messages of nationalism rather than integration."

**MICHELLE BACHELET**
President of Chile

"There are unquestionably bad trade practices by nations like China, but the better approach is targeted enforcement of those bad practices.

Our economy and our national security are strengthened by fostering free trade with our allies."

**SPEAKER PAUL D. RYAN**
Republican of Wisconsin

"A generalized tariff that would actually harm allies, harm American consumers, by the way, harm American workers that use steel in production, hurting their competitive nature in global markets as well, I'm opposed to that."

**SENATOR RON JOHNSON**
Republican of Wisconsin

"The idea that you can undermine core ally relationships, which have been the most enduring source of mutual defense, in the name of a national defense decision? It just doesn't make any sense."

**JACK LEW**
Former Treasury secretary

"I am against import duties in general, but the current rules make things very difficult. It's like competing in an Olympic race wearing lead shoes."

**ELON MUSK**
Chief executive of Tesla Motors

"The E.U. is a close ally of the U.S. and we continue to be of the view that the E.U. should be excluded from these measures."

**CECILIA MALMSTROM**
European Union trade commissioner

"The U.S. measures hit us where it hurts most. ... If we do not act immediately, Europe is at risk to lose a strategic industry."

**GERD GÖTZ**
Director General of European Aluminum

"We look forward to educating the Trump administration on the vital role the Japanese steel industry plays in the American marketplace. The Japanese industry is not part of the import problem but a solution."

**TADAAKI YAMAGUCHI**
Chairman of the Japan Steel Information Center

"Trump's actions are a challenge to the global steel sector and must be met with even broader opposition."

**CHINA IRON AND STEEL ASSOCIATION**

"This is a very important matter for Australia. It's also a very important matter of principle. So we're making contacts at every level throughout the administration, including business representatives, to make our case."

**JULIE BISHOP**
Australia's foreign minister

"If the worst case scenario happens, we are ready to take the U.S. to the WTO court, and we are discussing with other allies, other partners, to do it together."

**JYRKI KATAINEN**
European Union vice president for jobs and competitiveness

# U.S. Allies Sign Sweeping Trade Deal in Challenge to Trump

BY ERNESTO LONDOÑO AND MOTOKO RICH | MARCH 8, 2018

SANTIAGO, CHILE — A trade pact originally conceived by the United States to counter China's growing economic might in Asia now has a new target: President Trump's embrace of protectionism.

A group of 11 nations — including major United States allies like Japan, Canada and Australia — signed a broad trade deal on Thursday in Chile's capital, Santiago, that challenges Mr. Trump's view of trade as a zero-sum game filled with winners and losers.

Covering 500 million people on either side of the Pacific Ocean, the pact represents a new vision for global trade as the United States imposes steel and aluminum tariffs on even some of its closest friends.

Mr. Trump withdrew the United States from an earlier version of the agreement, then known as the Trans-Pacific Partnership, a year ago as one of his first acts in office. The resuscitated deal is undeniably weaker without the participation of the world's biggest economy, but it serves as a powerful sign of how countries that have previously counted on American leadership are now forging ahead without it.

"Globally, there has been an increasing level of uncertainty, given the adoption of policies and measures by some key players that question the principles that have contributed to generating prosperity for our peoples," President Michelle Bachelet of Chile said in a speech shortly before the pact was signed. "We need to stay on the course of globalization, yet learning from our past mistakes."

In its original incarnation as the TPP, the accord was conceived as a counterweight to China, whose vast economy was drawing other Asian countries closer despite its state-driven model and steep trade barriers. Not only does the pact lower trade barriers, it could also prod Beijing to make changes to enjoy the same benefits.

President Trump officially withdrawing the United States from the Trans-Pacific Partnership in January 2017.

When President Obama was advocating the deal, he said that "America should call the shots" instead of China.

Now, signatories are opening the door for China to join. Heraldo Muñoz, Chile's foreign minister, told reporters on Thursday afternoon that Chinese officials had been weighing the possibility of signing on.

"This will be open to anyone who accepts its components," Mr. Muñoz said. "It's not an agreement against anyone. It's in favor of open trade."

On Thursday, Mr. Trump went in the opposite direction, announcing tariffs on steel and aluminum imports to the United States. He said that Canada and Mexico were being exempted for now, and that allies like Australia could later be excluded. His order could affect Brazil, China, Germany, Japan, South Korea and Turkey, though he said he would have leeway to add or take countries off the list as he sees fit.

The United States has "gone from being a leader to actually being the No. 1 antagonist and No. 1 source of fear" on trade, said Jeffrey Wilson, the head of research at Perth U.S.-Asia Center at the University of Western Australia. "If you're a trade policy maker in Asia, your No. 1 fear is that Trump is going to take a swing at you."

He added that such fears could prompt countries, however reluctantly, to tether themselves more closely to China. "The U.S. is really delivering the region to China at the moment," Mr. Wilson said.

The new agreement — known as the Comprehensive and Progressive Agreement for Trans-Pacific Partnership — drops tariffs drastically and establishes sweeping new trade rules in markets that represent about a seventh of the world's economy. It opens more markets to free trade in agricultural products and digital services around the region. While American beef faces 38.5 percent tariffs in Japan, for example, beef from Australia, New Zealand and Canada will not.

Once it goes into effect, the agreement is expected to generate an additional $147 billion in global income, according to an analysis by the Peterson Institute for International Economics. Its backers say it also bolsters protections for intellectual property and includes language that could prod members to improve labor conditions.

Other members include Mexico, Vietnam, New Zealand, Chile, Malaysia, Peru, Singapore and Brunei. The deal will go into effect as soon as the legislative bodies of at least three signers ratify it. How long that will take is unclear.

China, which has discussed forming its own regional trade pact, has been more positive about the new deal since the United States pulled out. It sent a high-level delegation a year ago to Viña del Mar, Chile, where the pact's members sought to regroup after the United States' withdrawal. Experts said China could feel the pull if still more countries joined. The pact is also built around fostering trade in sophisticated manufactured goods and high-tech products, and China now produces many of those in abundance.

"It's hard to ignore rules that everyone else is agreeing to, and they will probably look carefully at these rules," said Wendy Cutler, a former United States trade negotiator who worked on the Trans-Pacific Partnership and is now managing director of the Washington office of the Asia Society Policy Institute.

Wang Yi, China's foreign minister, said on Thursday that the government hoped free-trade agreements in the region would play "a constructive role in their respective fields in resisting trade protectionism and building an open world economy."

The new version of the TPP does not pack the same punch as the earlier iteration. With the United States, the agreement would have represented 40 percent of the world's economy, giving its provisions added heft.

Still, the deal could appeal to companies trying to navigate the shifting trade waters.

"In a world that is so upside-down, especially for companies, companies will need to seek out growth and stability wherever they can," said Deborah Elms, founder and executive director of the Asian Trade Center, a consulting firm in Singapore. "And that stability does not appear to be coming from the United States, where policy seems to shift at a moment's notice."

Japan, which has the largest economy among the remaining trade partners and played a leadership role in keeping the coalition of 11 countries together, is still holding out hopes that the United States might return to the pact, under either Mr. Trump or a subsequent administration.

"We think the U.S. should come back, and we'll say, 'Please do come back,' " said Ichiro Fujisaki, a former Japanese ambassador to Washington. "It may sound a little impertinent, but the U.S. has taken many different positions on the economy or security."

The Trump administration has recently signaled that it is open to re-entering the Trans-Pacific Partnership. In an interview at the World Economic Forum earlier this year, Mr. Trump said, "If we did a substantially better deal, I would be open to TPP."

Steven Mnuchin, the United States Treasury secretary, said he had held discussions about the prospect of rekindling American membership in the pact, though at a congressional hearing in February, he said it was not a priority.

Yorizumi Watanabe, a professor of policy management at Keio University in Tokyo, said, "If the U.S. is retreating from this region, either as the pace setter or agenda setter of economic affairs or security affairs, this will be quite detrimental to the stability of this region."

He added: "TPP as such should not be seen as a mere free-trade or economic agreement. This should be seen from a kind of geopolitical point of view."

Heft could come from others. The Peterson Institute for International Economics in Washington estimates that if five other places — Indonesia, South Korea, the Philippines, Taiwan and Thailand — joined the partnership, the annual increase to global income would total $449 billion by 2030, almost as much as it would have been if the United States were included.

In the deal signed on Thursday, only 22 of more than 600 original provisions have been suspended, relating to intellectual property protection and a grab bag of other issues, several of which had been pushed by the United States. Kazuyoshi Umemoto, Japan's chief negotiator for the partnership, said that if the United States decided to re-enter the deal, those provisions could be reinstated.

"Trump won't last forever," said Patricio Navia, a political scientist at New York University. "Countries will return to a path toward globalization and this sends a beacon of hope."

# U.S. Allies Jostle to Win Exemptions From Trump Tariffs

BY JACK EWING | MARCH 9, 2018

FRANKFURT — South Korea made an impassioned appeal to the American secretary of defense and national security adviser, reminding them of its role trying to defang North Korea. Europe pointed out that it was, in fact, a longstanding military ally of the United States.

But it was Australia that deployed a secret weapon a day after President Trump signed an order imposing tariffs on steel and aluminum imports, as nations jockeyed for exemptions from the levies.

"We're calling in all contacts at every level," Julie Bishop, Australia's foreign minister, told the Australian Broadcasting Corporation. Top among those enlisted: the golfing legend Greg Norman, a friend of Mr. Trump's. "We will continue to push our case, we'll continue to advocate on behalf of Australia for as long as it takes," she said.

In seeking to win a respite from the tariffs, American allies tried a mix of persuasion and threats, personal appeals and diplomatic leverage. But they faced a delicate balancing act. A country that offers something in return for an exemption could set a precedent, allowing the White House to make further demands in the future in return for access to the United States market, and fracture any sense of unity between capitals from Brussels to Seoul that have roundly criticized the tariffs.

Questions over how to pressure Mr. Trump were similarly perilous. Nations trying to protect their own domestic steel and aluminum producers risked creating an every-nation-for-itself atmosphere, undermining the decades-old World Trade Organization system for resolving global trade disputes. But taking legal action could not only start a protracted process but also set off American ire.

"If you now start making concessions on other things, you give in to blackmail," said Guntram Wolff, the director of Bruegel, a research organization in Brussels. "I would reject that."

On Saturday, Cecilia Malmström, the European Union's trade commissioner, met with the United States trade representative, Robert Lighthizer, in Brussels, after a meeting that also included Japan to talk about steel overcapacity. There was no resolution of the tariffs issue, however.

European Union countries have been compiling a list of American products that could be subject to reciprocal levies. The provisional list correlated strongly with Republican congressional districts and included Harley-Davidson motorcycles, bourbon, rice, kidney beans, sweet corn, tobacco and peanut butter.

The region is likely to face a tough decision, however, about whether to wait for World Trade Organization approval, a lengthy process, or simply to impose the retaliatory sanctions. Ms. Malmström said during a news conference in Brussels on Wednesday that any fight back against the United States would be "by the book."

But even as European Union leaders prepared for retaliatory action, they also recalled the long history of trans-Atlantic bonhomie.

Brigitte Zypries, the German economics minister, wrote in a letter to Wilbur Ross, the United States commerce secretary, that Europe and America should work together to address the real problem: a global glut of steel production that has driven down prices.

"We need trans-Atlantic solidarity on this issue, and not trade conflicts," she said.

Still, there were signs that attempts by some countries to win tariff immunity from the United States were sowing tension among European allies.

Liam Fox, Britain's international trade secretary, told the BBC on Friday he would "be looking to see how we can maximize the U.K.'s case for exemption" when he visits Washington next week. The suggestion that Britain might go its own way provoked a rebuke from Jyrki Katainen, European Union vice president for jobs and competitiveness. "We cannot accept that the E.U. is divided to different categories," Mr. Katainen said Friday.

Australia had already shown how to win Mr. Trump's favor with an energetic lobbying effort that seems to be paying off. The president, who excluded Canada and Mexico from the tariffs, singled out Australia on Thursday as another country that could be exempt.

Ms. Bishop, the Australian foreign minister, said she had been in contact with Secretary of State Rex W. Tillerson while he had been traveling in Africa. She also said she had spoken with close business contacts of Mr. Trump. And she made her case to Nikki Haley, the United States ambassador to the United Nations, while in New York this week.

Australia also deployed Mr. Norman, the golfer known as the Great White Shark, who has been effusive in his praise of his friend Mr. Trump.

Mr. Norman and a handful of other prominent Australian business leaders signed a letter beseeching Mr. Trump not to take "any action that might have demonstrable negative impact on the mutually beneficial American-Australian bilateral relationship."

The efforts may be paying off. On Friday, Mr. Trump said on Twitter that he had spoken to the country's prime minister, Malcolm Turnbull. "Working very quickly on a security agreement so we don't have to impose steel or aluminum tariffs on our ally, the great nation of Australia," he said.

South Korean envoys appealed for their own exemption when they visited the White House this week to brief Mr. Trump on their meeting with North Korea's leader, Kim Jong-un. The meeting set the stage for Mr. Trump to agree to meet Mr. Kim for negotiations on North Korea's nuclear arsenal.

The envoys urged Secretary of Defense James N. Mattis and H.R. McMaster, Mr. Trump's national security adviser, to intervene for the sake of the alliance, said Kim Eui-kyeom, the spokesman for South Korean President Moon Jae-in.

Whether the appeals will work is an open question. Despite South Korea's critical role in defusing tensions with North Korea, the Trump administration has claimed the country is a conduit for Chinese steel evading anti-dumping rules — a practice known as transshipping. South Korean officials have argued that only 2.4 percent of steel exported to the United States in 2016 used Chinese material.

Seoul is badly in need of a free pass for its steel industry. The country accounts for almost 10 percent of United States steel imports and stands to suffer the most from tariffs.

That highlights another problem with Mr. Trump's protectionist thrust: Most of the producers hurt are friends, or at least thought they were.

"The difficulty is that a huge portion of U.S. steel imports come from core allies like Nafta, Japan, Australia, and Brazil," said Seth Rosenfeld, an analyst at Jefferies, an investment bank, in London. "The U.S. will be in a situation where it is granting Japan an exemption and not Korea and this has the risk of royally disrupting your geopolitics."

American allies were particularly floored by Mr. Trump's justification for the tariffs. He invoked a provision of W.T.O. rules that allows countries to impose trade restrictions in the interest of national security.

"How India or any other country could be a threat to the U.S. within the steel industry, I don't know," said Shivramkrishnan Hariharan, the commercial director of Essar Steel, a large steel manufacturer based in Mumbai.

The national security argument seemed even weaker when applied to South Korea or European countries that have formal military alliances with the United States.

The tariffs "have nothing to do with the security of the United States," Georg Streiter, a spokesman for German Chancellor Angela Merkel, said at a news briefing Friday. "It's purely business."

Argentina's president, Mauricio Macri, made his country's request for an exemption in a Friday morning phone call to Mr. Trump. Mr. Macri expressed "his concern over the potential negative effect of these measures," the Argentine government said. "Trump expressed a commitment to evaluate his request."

Argentina is already paying a price for United States trade barriers. Last year, the Department of Commerce imposed duties of up to 70 percent on Argentine biodiesel, virtually shutting off what had been the most lucrative market for the country's soybean-based biofuel.

While foreign officials said they hoped to use diplomacy to win exemptions to the steel and aluminum tariffs, they also reserved the right to get nasty. The European Union, South Korea and others said they would file complaints with the W.T.O., which under international treaties has the power to resolve trade disputes.

Among them was Brazil, which sends steel products to the United States but also imported about $1 billion in American coal last year for its metals industry.

Jorge Arbache, the Brazilian planning ministry's secretary for foreign affairs, said in an interview that the Brazilian government was still trying to work things out in a friendly way.

But he noted that his country retained some options, including appealing to the W.T.O., or reducing its purchases from the United States.

"If we produce less steel," Mr. Arbache said, "we may import less American coal."

# Trump's Tariffs Trigger Global Chain Reaction to Halt Imports

BY ANA SWANSON, ALAN RAPPEPORT AND IAN AUSTEN | MARCH 27, 2018

WASHINGTON — The Trump administration's steel and aluminum tariffs are provoking a chain reaction around the globe, as governments from Europe to Canada prepare to erect barriers to prevent cheap metal once bound for the United States from entering their markets.

On Tuesday, Prime Minister Justin Trudeau of Canada announced a series of regulatory changes that would make it easier for border officials to block steel and aluminum imports into that nation. The European Union has begun a "safeguard investigation" that could result in tariffs or other trade actions if it determines that steel intended for the American market is being diverted to the bloc.

"These past few days, we've looked at strengthening the measures that we already have in place because it's important that we not be taking in dumped steel from around the world," Mr. Trudeau told reporters in Ottawa.

Foreign policymakers have long shared President Trump's concerns about cheap foreign steel flooding their markets, particularly from China. But Mr. Trump's stiff 25 percent steel tariffs and 10 percent aluminum tariffs, which will halt the flow of foreign metals into the United States, have prompted other countries to move more rapidly to curtail overseas imports.

The response could help Mr. Trump claim victory on one of his primary trade goals: cutting down on a glut of cheap Chinese steel, including metals that are routed through other countries through a process known as transshipping.

This month, Mr. Trump called transshipping "a big deal" and argued that China routes much more steel to the United States than the statistics show. Administration officials have contended that Chinese steel is lightly processed and shipped through other countries, but they have been unable to quantify the pervasiveness of this practice.

The American metals industry has long claimed that it is powerless against an onslaught of cheap metal from China, which now produces roughly half of the world's steel and aluminum. Companies argue that past efforts to get China to reduce overcapacity have largely failed and that the only recourse is taking broader action that could galvanize a global movement.

Scott N. Paul, the head of the Alliance for American Manufacturing and a supporter of the tariffs, said countries were taking initial steps toward a series of agreements and discussions that could help to squeeze out overcapacity and anticompetitive practices.

"Other large steel countries and blocs will necessarily step up to the plate and take a tougher line with China and on transshipment and circumvention. I think you see that occurring in the E.U. with its safeguard investigation, and I think you see that with respect to the Canadian government," he said. "I don't think this is by any means the conclusion of the process. I think it's just getting started."

By restricting the supply of foreign metals in the United States, the tariffs are meant to raise the domestic price of those metals, which will translate into profits for struggling American metal makers. But in the process, more cheap metal will be available in markets outside the United States. That will push down the global price of steel and aluminum and create a two-tiered market.

After Mr. Trump announced his tariffs, trade unions and Canada's steel and aluminum industries warned Mr. Trudeau that, without its own measures, Canada could be flooded with cheap steel and aluminum from countries that export at artificially low prices.

European officials have also argued that, without protections, their companies could become collateral damage. Officials in Brussels have warned that they will take "safeguard measures" in the form of additional tariffs on steel products if an inquiry into the American tariffs shows there could be a significant surge in cheap steel imports.

"The E.U. is more than an innocent bystander," said Fredrik Erixon, the director for the European Center for International Political Economy, a think tank based in Brussels.

The European Union already has "antidumping" tariffs on steel in place, mainly directed toward cheap Chinese imports. But the bloc's leaders have also made clear they are prepared to do more and to exert diplomatic pressure on Beijing, pushing China to reduce government subsidies for its steel sector, cut import tariffs and open its market to American and European steel.

Some supporters of the tariffs see the moves as evidence that the Trump administration's strategy is working. But other trade experts see this chain reaction as the first in a damaging series of actions that will end up raising the price of metals globally and making markets around the world less free.

Eswar Prasad, a professor of trade policy at Cornell University, said that although Mr. Trump's approach appeared to be bearing fruit in the short term, it could ultimately hurt the trust of American trading partners and hamper the economy.

"Even if it looks like other countries are lining up on the U.S. side, and this is going to help in terms of reducing steel and aluminum supply, it may do very little for employment in those industries, and it may end up hurting other industries that use steel and aluminum as imports," he said. "So we could end up with a somewhat Pyrrhic victory for the United States."

For decades, the United States has been a primary driver in pushing to remove trade barriers globally, believing that these changes would increase trade and lift wealth around the world. The Trump administration has taken a drastically different approach, arguing that these beliefs have devastated domestic manufacturing and that tariffs and other restrictions are necessary to protect the American market from unfair trade practices.

Despite the president's initial statements that the measure would apply to all countries, Canada, Mexico, members of the European

Union, Australia, Argentina, South Korea and Brazil have been exempted from the steel and aluminum tariffs. Together, the countries accounted for nearly two-thirds of American steel and aluminum imports last year.

The tariffs now fall on exporters that sent roughly $18 billion in steel and aluminum to the United States in 2017 — mainly Russia, China, Japan, the United Arab Emirates, Taiwan, Turkey, Vietnam and India, according to research by Chad P. Bown, a senior fellow at the Peterson Institute for International Economics.

On Tuesday, Mr. Trump continued to push for global pressure on China during telephone calls with Chancellor Angela Merkel of Germany and President Emmanuel Macron of France. In both discussions, according to official readouts released by the White House, Mr. Trump raised China's unfair trading practices and its "illegal" acquisition of intellectual property.

# Mexico, Hitting Back, Imposes Tariffs on $3 Billion Worth of U.S. Goods

BY ANA SWANSON AND JIM TANKERSLEY | JUNE 5, 2018

WASHINGTON — Mexico hit back at the United States on Tuesday, imposing tariffs on around $3 billion worth of American pork, steel, cheese and other goods in response to the Trump administration's steel and aluminum levies, further straining relations between the two countries as they struggle to rewrite the North American Free Trade Agreement.

The tariffs, which were announced last week, came into effect as the Trump administration threw yet another complication into the fractious Nafta talks. Officials are now saying they want to splinter discussions with Canada and Mexico and work on separate agreements rather than continue three-country discussions to rewrite the 1994 trade deal.

Larry Kudlow, President Trump's chief economic adviser, said on Tuesday that Mr. Trump's "preference now, and he asked me to convey this, is to actually negotiate with Mexico and Canada separately."

Mr. Kudlow, speaking on "Fox and Friends," said pursuing separate deals might allow an agreement to be reached "more rapidly," adding: "I think that's the key point. You know, Nafta has kind of dragged on."

The Trump administration hit Mexico and Canada with 25 percent steel tariffs and 10 percent aluminum tariffs on June 1 as part of a campaign to pressure the countries to agree to America's demands on a revised Nafta. The United States also imposed metals tariffs on the European Union, Japan and other countries as part of an effort to stop the flow of imported metals, which the administration has said threatens national security by degrading the American industrial base.

The trade approach has only inflamed allies, including Canada and Mexico, which have threatened to strike back with their own targeted tariffs aimed at Republican states and areas that supported Mr. Trump.

Mexico's list was designed to hit at parts of the United States represented by high-profile Republicans, Mexican officials have said, including steel from Vice President Mike Pence's home state of Indiana, motorboats from Senator Marco Rubio's Florida, and agricultural products from the California district of Representative Kevin McCarthy, the House majority leader.

Farmers, who are among those most vulnerable to the Mexican tariffs, said the tariffs would devastate American agriculture. "These tariffs will exact immediate and painful consequences on many American farmers," Angela Hofmann, deputy director of Farmers for Free Trade, said in a statement. "Hog, apple, potato and dairy farmers are among those suddenly facing a 10 or 20 percent tax hike on the exports they depend of for their livelihoods. Farmers need certainty and open markets to make ends meet. Right now they are getting chaos and protectionism."

It is unclear which country will blink first, leaving the future of the trade deal, and the millions of jobs across the continent that are linked to it, so uncertain that many companies are withholding investments they might make to take advantage of the pact.

Mr. Kudlow insisted that the president was not planning to withdraw from Nafta — which he has frequently threatened to do. However, splitting the current trilateral deal into two separate bilateral agreements would likely require nullifying the 25-year-old agreement.

On Friday, Mr. Trump said he would be interested in pursuing separate deals. "These are two very different countries," he said.

"I like free trade, but I want fair trade," Mr. Trump said, adding, "They cannot believe they've gotten away with this for so many decades."

People familiar with the deliberations say the idea of separate talks is aimed at pressuring Canada, which American negotiators see as obstructionist and an impediment to the progress of the Nafta negotiations. The preference for bilateral negotiations has also emerged as one of the sole areas of agreement among Mr. Trump's warring trade advisers, who agree on little else but the ability to extract bigger concessions through one-on-one talks. Bilateral deals are also a longtime focus of the president.

American officials say that splitting the negotiations could help the United States take advantage of what could be a short and crucial window to negotiate with the current government of Mexico, which could be ousted in national elections in July, and replaced by a government that is less inclined to cut a deal with the Trump administration.

However, both Mexico and Canada insist that the idea is a non-starter.

Mexican negotiators say they would not be willing to consider splitting the negotiations, a move they view as potentially damaging to North American supply chains and an unnecessary complication of a pact that many businesses rely on, according to people familiar with their thinking.

They add that they do not view Canada as their biggest problem in the talks. The three countries have remained at an impasse over significant provisions, including manufacturing rules for autos and an American proposal for a five-year sunset clause that would cause the deal to automatically expire unless the countries voted to renew it.

The clock has essentially run out for the administration to secure a Nafta deal this year. The Trump administration had been trying to conclude Nafta talks by the end of May in order to submit the deal for a vote in the current Republican-controlled Congress.

Given the statutory deadlines the administration must meet to get a trade deal approved, it now appears likely that any vote would drag into next year, after midterm elections that could shift the political makeup of Congress.

Mr. Trump's strategy in the negotiations with Canada and Mexico has drawn criticism from the business community as well as Democrats and Republicans.

A spokeswoman for Representative Kevin Brady of Texas, the chairman of the Ways and Means Committee, said Tuesday that Mr. Brady opposed splitting the negotiations in two.

"A Nafta without both Canada and Mexico included is no longer a North American Free Trade Agreement," the spokeswoman, Julia Slingsby, said. "Chairman Brady believes one free trade agreement with Canada and Mexico is best for America. It provides the most certainty for American companies and is the best way we can sell 'Made in America' products."

And a survey of chief executive officers released Tuesday morning by Business Roundtable showed that while executives have a positive view of the economy, they see the administration's trade policy and the prospect of retaliation from other countries as an escalating risk to their businesses.

Joshua Bolten, the president of Business Roundtable, said that uncertainties about trade policy were "a growing weight on economic progress — especially amid escalating trade tensions. America's current and future economic vitality depends on productive talks with China and a successful modernization of Nafta."

Privately, some congressional Republicans expressed an openness to the administration negotiating some trade issues bilaterally with Mexico and with China. But they expressed little support for scrapping Nafta entirely and replacing it with separate deals.

"Now is the time to stay the course and work with our trading partners to find a path forward on an updated Nafta that will meet the high-standards of bipartisan TPA and gain the support of Congress," Senator Orrin G. Hatch of Utah, the chairman of the Finance Committee, said on Twitter.

# Anger Flares as G-7 Heads to Quebec

BY MICHAEL D. SHEAR | JUNE 7, 2018

WASHINGTON — President Trump will skip most of the second day of a summit meeting with allies this weekend, the White House said late Thursday, as he engaged in a contentious war of words over trade on the eve of a gathering that will underscore his isolation from the leaders of the world's largest economies.

Sarah Huckabee Sanders, the White House press secretary, announced that Mr. Trump will leave Canada at 10:30 a.m. Saturday, well before scheduled sessions on climate change, clean energy and oceans. He will attend an early-morning session on "women's empowerment," but he will be gone before any joint statement is issued by the other leaders.

Earlier Thursday, President Emmanuel Macron of France and Prime Minister Justin Trudeau of Canada lashed out at Mr. Trump for

STEPHEN CROWLEY/THE NEW YORK TIMES

President Trump with other leaders of the Group of 7 last year for what is referred to as the "family photo." This year's may not feature many smiles.

imposing tariffs on their steel and aluminum industries. They called it an illegal economic assault on their countries that is unanimously opposed by the other leaders of the Group of 7 who will gather Friday in a sleepy village in Quebec for their annual summit meeting.

"The American President may not mind being isolated, but neither do we mind signing a 6 country agreement if need be," Mr. Macron said Thursday in an especially acerbic tweet. "Because these 6 countries represent values, they represent an economic market which has the weight of history behind it and which is now a true international force."

Mr. Trudeau said at a news conference with Mr. Macron that "we are going to defend our industries and our workers" and "show the U.S. president that his unacceptable actions are hurting his own citizens."

Mr. Trump responded with his trademark Twitter bluntness a few hours later, signaling that he has no intention of relenting on his aggressive trade demands and cares little about the diplomatic niceties that usually constrain public disagreements between the leaders of friendly nations.

"Please tell Prime Minister Trudeau and President Macron that they are charging the U.S. massive tariffs and create non-monetary barriers," the American president wrote. "The EU trade surplus with the U.S. is $151 Billion, and Canada keeps our farmers and others out."

He added, with a hint of sarcasm: "Look forward to seeing them tomorrow."

Mr. Trump was scheduled to arrive Friday morning at the meeting for a gathering that traditionally includes a moment of global camaraderie — the "family photo" that captures presidents and prime ministers smiling for the camera.

This year, there will not be many grins.

Mr. Trump is the black sheep of this family, the estranged sibling who decided to pick fights with his relatives just before arriving to dinner. The dispute, Larry Kudlow, the president's top economic adviser, acknowledges, is "much like a family quarrel," but with the potential for vast diplomatic and economic consequences for the world.

The anger of American allies, over Mr. Trump's decision to impose tariffs, is palpable.

"Patently absurd" is what Liam Fox, the British trade minister, called them. Chancellor Angela Merkel of Germany said they were "illegal," while Mr. Trudeau said they were "insulting and totally unacceptable" — and that was in the carefully worded public statement. In a phone call with Mr. Trump, he was said to be even more blunt.

Before the summit meeting, finance ministers from the other six countries that form the Group of 7, or G-7, condemned Mr. Trump's trade decisions in an extraordinary rebuke of a member nation's president. And some of the leaders themselves have threatened to boycott the usual end-of-meeting communiqué. A senior Canadian official said a statement by only Mr. Trudeau, the gathering's host, is possible.

Asked about the upcoming discussions in Canada, Ms. Merkel, the famously taciturn leader of Germany, said they would be "difficult."

There have been disagreements within the G-7 in the past, including a long chill between the Europeans and President George W. Bush over the Iraq war. When President Ronald Reagan put missiles in Europe, his counterparts branded him a cowboy who would start World War III.

But rarely — if ever — has there been the kind of visceral and unanimous outrage at an American president among the United States' most important allies, who for decades have seen the closest of relationships with the leader of the free world as a paramount foreign policy priority.

Mr. Trump has repeatedly poked his counterparts in the eye — ignoring their pleas to remain a part of the Paris climate treaty, the Trans-Pacific Partnership trade pact and the Iran nuclear deal, and more recently by branding their steel and aluminum industries threats to national security, and therefore subject to tariffs.

So when Mr. Trump disembarks Friday morning from Air Force One for a day and a half of closed-door meetings in the resort town of La Malbaie, the president can expect a subzero reception for what some observers have begun calling the "G6+1," a reference to the political and diplomatic isolation that Mr. Trump has created for himself with his unilateral trade and security actions against his friends.

Cliff Kupchan, a veteran foreign policy analyst, said he expected a "very frosty dynamic" and predicted that Mr. Trump is "going to get an earful from all of them." Dan Price, who guided Mr. Bush through many economic summit meetings, said the other six leaders should express their concerns to Mr. Trump, "even at the risk of offending a notoriously thin-skinned president."

And Mark Dubowitz, the chief executive of the Foundation for Defense of Democracies, said that because of "real indignation and real frustration" on the part of European leaders who are extremely angry at Mr. Trump, the "venting process is likely to continue" throughout the meeting.

The ill will among the United States' allies is a striking contrast to the praise Mr. Trump has heaped on North Korea, one of the country's most enduring adversaries, before his historic meeting next week with Kim Jong-un, the country's normally reclusive leader.

The president, who is scheduled to fly Saturday to Singapore from Quebec for the meeting, has called Mr. Kim — the leader of a country once described as part of an "axis of evil" — a "very honorable" man, even as he clashes repeatedly with his counterparts in the world's longest-lasting democracies.

Mr. Trump's feud with the allies is also risking a go-it-alone approach to China's trade practices, even as many trade experts have called for a unified front by Western economies to confront China. The disputes with the United States have frustrated European leaders, who are eager for a joint effort that might pressure Beijing for change. Leaders had hoped to use the meeting to help formulate a strategy to combat China's surplus steel, but they now appear more likely to focus on their own trade divisions instead.

"The isolation from our G-7 allies undermines the United States' ability to work with them to confront real challenges in Russia or China or the Middle East," Mr. Price said. "I certainly hope the president and his team will take the opportunity presented by the G-7 summit to find a path forward."

Others are less sanguine about that possibility.

Mr. Trump's decision to abandon the Iran deal was particularly infuriating to leaders in Europe, where businesses and banks had been eager to begin commercial activities in Iran with the lifting of sanctions. But because the president decided to withdraw the United States from the agreement, European businesses are likely to avoid doing business in Iran for fear of risking sanctions that could keep them out of the much more lucrative American markets.

"There's no underestimating the level of anger and frustration," Mr. Dubowitz said. "For the Europeans, this is really a question of sovereignty. It's a direct challenge, in the case of Iran, to their national security."

Still, the more immediate source of friction with Mr. Trump is on trade. Efforts to renegotiate the North American Free Trade Agreement have stalled in bitter disagreement. And the decision by the United States to claim national security concerns has infuriated even the most stalwart allies, who view it as a transparent — and ridiculous — attempt to get around the rules set by the World Trade Organization.

Mr. Trump has sent no signals that he is willing to back off. In remarks to reporters on Wednesday, Mr. Kudlow insisted that the president does not intend to be constrained by the global trading rules set up by his predecessors.

"That system has been broken in the last 20 years-plus. The World Trade Organization, for example, has become completely ineffectual," he said, adding later: "International multilateral organizations are not going to determine American policy. I think the president has made that very clear."

The allies at the G-7 are unlikely to give in, either. The Canadians and the European Union have filed cases against the United States at the World Trade Organization, and they have announced retaliatory tariffs in a tit-for-tat series of economic moves that could set off an all-out trade war.

French officials say Mr. Macron is likely to urge Mr. Trump to relent, arguing that Mr. Trump will damage the United States economy if he persists. Other allies are hoping that American businesses will pressure Mr. Trump to back off once the tariffs begin affecting their supply chains and profits.

Clues to how the meetings in Canada have gone may be found in the body language of Mr. Trump and his counterparts as they pose for pictures before and after their sessions.

Mr. Kupchan said he will be looking for the expressions on the faces of the allies: "Merkel sitting next to Trump, having just talked about Iran, with a massive frown, looking the other way," he said. "That's my best bet."

# Trump Refuses to Sign G-7 Statement and Calls Trudeau 'Weak'

BY MICHAEL D. SHEAR AND CATHERINE PORTER  |  JUNE 9, 2018

QUEBEC CITY — President Trump upended two days of global economic diplomacy late Saturday, refusing to sign a joint statement with America's allies, threatening to escalate his trade war on the country's neighbors and deriding Canada's prime minister as "very dishonest and weak."

In a remarkable pair of acrimony-laced tweets from aboard Air Force One as he flew away from the Group of 7 summit toward a meeting with North Korea's leader, Mr. Trump lashed out at Justin Trudeau. He accused the prime minister, who hosted the seven-nation gathering, of making false statements.

Literally moments after Mr. Trudeau's government proudly released the joint statement, noting it had been agreed to by all seven countries, Mr. Trump blew apart the veneer of cordiality that had prevailed throughout the two days of meetings in a resort town on the banks of the St. Lawrence River.

"Based on Justin's false statements at his news conference, and the fact that Canada is charging massive Tariffs to our U.S. farmers, workers and companies, I have instructed our U.S. Reps not to endorse the Communique as we look at Tariffs on automobiles flooding the U.S. Market!" Mr. Trump wrote.

A few hours earlier, Mr. Trudeau said the seven nations had reached broad agreements on a range of economic and foreign policy goals. But he acknowledged that deep disagreements remained between Mr. Trump and the leaders of the other nations, especially on trade.

Mr. Trudeau had sought to play down personal clashes with Mr. Trump as he wrapped up the summit, calling the meeting "very successful" and saying he was "inspired by the discussion." But he also pledged to retaliate against the United States tariffs on steel and aluminum products in defense of Canadian workers.

Mr. Trump, who apparently saw Mr. Trudeau's news conference on television aboard Air Force One, was clearly enraged.

"PM Justin Trudeau of Canada acted so meek and mild during our @g7 meetings," Mr. Trump said in a second tweet, "only to give a news conference after I left saying that, 'US Tariffs were kind of insulting' and he 'will not be pushed around.' Very dishonest & weak. Our Tariffs are in response to his of 270% on dairy!"

Not long after, John Bolton, the president's national security adviser, tweeted out a dramatic photo of Mr. Trump, arms crossed and scowling, looking defiant as the leaders of the other nations stood in a circle around him.

"Just another #G7 where other countries expect America will always be their bank," Mr. Bolton wrote as the president's plane stopped for refueling at Souda Bay on the Greek island of Crete. "The President made it clear today. No more."

Mr. Trudeau's office responded to the president's Twitter barrage with a carefully worded statement.

"We are focused on everything we accomplished here at the summit," said Cameron Ahmad, a spokesman for Mr. Trudeau. "The prime minister said nothing he hasn't said before — both in public, and in private conversations with the President."

The president's outburst had been foreshadowed for days leading up to the Canada summit, with Mr. Trump and his counterparts trading sharp-edged barbs that included threats of punches and counterpunches on tariffs. President Emmanuel Macron of France accused Mr. Trump of being willing to remain isolated from the world.

That was followed by 48 hours of tense and often confrontational closed-door discussions between Mr. Trump and the leaders of America's closest allies — France, Britain, Canada, Japan, Italy and Germany — in the hopes of resolving a brewing trade war among friends.

Instead, the gathering apparently served to further inflame Mr. Trump's belief that the United States is being treated unfairly by countries with which prior presidents had long ago negotiated trade agreements for the flow of goods and services.

The result was a slow-rolling collapse of the fragile alliances that officials at the summit — and even Mr. Trump's own White House advisers — insisted throughout the day could be maintained in the face of fundamental disagreements.

Reporters on Air Force One had been told that the United States would sign the joint statement. And minutes after the president's tweets, reporters were sent an email that had clearly been prepared earlier touting Mr. Trump's participation in the summit, complete with photos.

Earlier in the day, before Mr. Trump left the summit, he brought up the dramatic prospect of completely eliminating tariffs on goods and services, even as he threatened to end all trade with them if they didn't stop what he said were unfair trade practices.

Mr. Trump, speaking to reporters at the end of the contentious meeting, said that eliminating all trading barriers would be "the ultimate thing." He railed about what he called "ridiculous and unacceptable" tariffs on American goods and vowed to end them.

"It's going to stop," he said, "or we'll stop trading with them. And that's a very profitable answer, if we have to do it." He added, "We're like the piggy bank that everybody's robbing — and that ends."

The other six leaders were defiant in the face of Mr. Trump's threats.

"I have made it very clear to the president that it is not something we relish doing, but it is something that we absolutely will do," Mr. Trudeau said. "As Canadians, we are polite, we're reasonable, but also we will not be pushed around."

Mr. Macron said the trade debates at the summit were "sometimes quite heated." Asked who won the tug-of-war with Trump, Mr. Macron said: "There is no winner, there are only losers when you take that strategy."

Theresa May, the British prime minister, blasted Mr. Trump's tariffs. She said she had registered "our deep disappointment at the unjustified decision" and that the loss of trade through tariffs would "ultimately make everyone poorer."

The president's public comments on trade Saturday echoed the complaints he made directly to the leaders from Canada, Japan and Europe in private sessions on Friday. Mr. Trump confronted several of the leaders individually, giving examples of how, in his view, each of their countries had mistreated the United States, whether it be through trade barriers or security commitments, according to a European official.

The president delivered a running monologue in one of the closed-door meetings, one person familiar with the discussion said. One minute, he slammed Germany for taking advantage of the United States by selling so many cars there. The next, he talked about how his grandfather was German and how much he loved Europe.

Several of the leaders responded aggressively to Mr. Trump's demands — as they have repeatedly done in public — listing their own complaints about American tariffs and other trade measures, the official said. Several countries have said that they will retaliate against the United States' new steel and aluminum tariffs with increased tariffs of their own.

"If they retaliate, they're making a mistake," Mr. Trump said on Saturday.

Mr. Trump's surprise proposal for a tariff-free G7 followed from a conversation the president had on Air Force One heading to Canada with Larry Kudlow, his national economic adviser. Mr. Kudlow, a self-described "lifelong free trader," wrote an op-ed article in The Washington Post on Thursday saying that he did not prefer tariffs but that Mr. Trump's actions were "a wake-up call to the dangers of a broken trading system that is increasingly unfree."

Mr. Trump and Mr. Kudlow discussed the article on the plane, but the president surprised even his own team by raising the idea with the other leaders. While some observers took it as more of a talking point, a senior administration official said the president was serious about it and wanted it given serious study. Other leaders, the official said, expressed interest.

The official spoke on the condition of anonymity to describe closed-door discussions.

Asked late Saturday what he told Mr. Trump about the surprise proposal for a tariff-free zone, Mr. Macron said, with a smile: "Be my guest, if that's your wish."

Throughout his remarks on Saturday, Mr. Trump repeatedly returned to his broader complaints about trade practices around the world, insisting that it was the fault of past American leaders who had agreed to deals that benefited other countries more than the United States.

He complained that American dairy farmers were being treated unfairly by Canada.

"The United States pays tremendous tariffs on dairy, as an example, 270 percent," he said. "Nobody knows that."

"We don't want to pay anything," he said. "Why should we pay?"

The president also said American farmers had been hurt for a long time by trade barriers that made it harder for them to sell their goods to other countries.

"You look at our farmers," he said. "For 15 years, the graph has gone just like this: down."

"I blame our leaders," Mr. Trump said. "In fact, I congratulate the leaders of other countries for so crazily being able to make these trade deals that were so good for their country and so bad for the United States. But those days are over."

Mr. Trump said some of the other leaders he met with during the summit appeared to admit that their trade arrangements with the United States were unfair.

"A lot of these countries actually smile at me when I'm talking," he said. "And the smile is, 'We couldn't believe we got away with it.'"

That assessment by Mr. Trump stands in contrast to the public statements by those leaders, who have repeatedly insisted that they will not accept the kinds of tariffs that Mr. Trump has imposed on their industries.

In addition to trade, Mr. Trump also took questions about his call for Russia to be reinstated as a member of the Group of 7 nations, despite having been expelled four years ago in the wake of the Russian annexation of Crimea.

"I would rather see Russia in the G-8 as opposed to the G-7," he said. "I would say that the G-8 is a more meaningful group than the G-7. Absolutely."

# CHAPTER 4

# Escalation and Consequences

In the aftermath of new tariffs and changes to trade agreements imposed by President Trump, many economists said a trade war was inevitable. A trade war occurs when one nation imposes tariffs and quotas on imports, and other countries retaliate with similar restrictions. It escalates to the point where it affects all international trade, and nations trying to protect their own economies may end up depressing them in the long run. Economists around the world are watching the United States to see if its actions will, indeed, spark a trade war.

## Trump Embraces a Trade War, Which Could Undermine Growth

BY JIM TANKERSLEY  |  MARCH 2, 2018

WASHINGTON — After a year of delighting conservatives with tax cuts and regulatory rollbacks, President Trump is finally following through on the type of trade crackdowns that terrify Republican leaders in Congress and many economists. They warn that the trade war Mr. Trump appears eager to launch could backfire, sending America and the world into recession.

Mr. Trump said on Thursday that he would soon levy tariffs on imported steel and aluminum from every foreign country, a move that sent stocks tumbling through the end of the day. On Friday, he ramped

Coke conveyors stand near the blast furnaces at U.S. Steel's Granite City Works in Granite City, Ill.

up his rhetoric in the face of criticism, saying on Twitter that "trade wars are good, and easy to win."

When a country (USA) is losing many billions of dollars on trade with virtually every country it does business with, trade wars are good, and easy to win. Example, when we are down $100 billion with a certain country and they get cute, don't trade anymore-we win big. It's easy!

— Donald J. Trump (@realDonaldTrump) Mar 2, 2018

Many economists say the opposite: that even the prospect of a trade war will hurt the economic expansion that is underway and that Mr. Trump loves to take credit for.

"Industries that buy steel and aluminum, not to mention agricultural exporters, employ many times more people than the industries that the president wants to protect," said Peter A. Petri, an economist and trade expert at Brandeis University's International Business School. "Whether we go through with his approach is anyone's guess, but business investment depends on predictable policy, and relentless chaos takes its toll even if cooler heads prevail on the policies that the president is tweeting about."

The planned tariffs are stiff: 25 percent for steel and 10 percent for aluminum. They appear likely to buoy domestic investment and, to some degree, job creation in those industries, while raising prices on consumers and squeezing other industries that rely heavily on metals, such as automobile manufacturing and beverage production. They were hailed by labor groups, whose workers have seen their jobs shipped overseas, liberal economists and lawmakers, while criticized by business groups such as the National Retail Federation.

On their own, the tariffs appear unlikely to affect growth or inflation to a great degree, economists said. Mr. Trump's tariffs "would by themselves have only a small macroeconomic impact," said Mark Zandi, the chief economist at Moody's Analytics and a vocal critic of Mr. Trump's trade agenda during the campaign. Mr. Zandi said they were likely to add not quite 0.1 percentage points to inflation, which is currently hovering just under 2 percent, and to reduce economic growth by only a few hundredths of a percentage point.

What worries many economists, particularly on Wall Street, is the prospect that Mr. Trump is set to launch a broader trade war. The national security grounds he is invoking as rationale for the tariffs could provoke swift retaliation from trading partners such as Canada, which will be affected far more by the measures than China will.

"This is likely to escalate trade tensions," economists at Goldman Sachs wrote on Thursday, "particularly as it looks likely to apply to a broad group of countries including to some allies of the U.S. We expect further disruptive trade developments over the coming months."

The tariffs could also bring condemnation from the World Trade Organization — and a potentially dramatic showdown if the United States ignores rulings from the group, which has been marginalized by the Trump administration.

If such problems spiral worldwide, Mr. Zandi said, "a particularly dark scenario could end in a global trade war. The economic fallout from such a war could be serious, ending in a global recession."

Other liberal economists caution that such a scenario remains unlikely. "I'd expect some counter-tariffs on our exports, maybe from China on food products" as a result of the tariffs, said Jared Bernstein, a former Obama administration economist who is now at the Center on Budget and Policy Priorities. "You always hear trade war at these moments. That doesn't mean that's always wrong, but it usually is."

From the beginning of his insurgent 2016 presidential campaign, Mr. Trump has seen "winning" on trade — measured by reducing bilateral trade deficits, particularly with China, the trading partner Mr. Trump is most concerned with — as critical for boosting the economy. Reducing trade deficits, he has argued, will work in tandem with lowering taxes and reducing federal regulations, to supercharge growth.

Mr. Trump took several steps last year to freeze or roll back regulations, and he signed a $1.5 trillion tax-cut bill in December. He also took initial steps to reorient trade policy, pulling out of the Trans-Pacific Partnership and embarking on a fractious renegotiation of the North American Free Trade Agreement. But while economic growth accelerated, the trade deficit in goods and services widened to $566 billion for the year, the largest amount since 2008. The goods deficit with China hit $375 billion, a record.

The tariffs Mr. Trump announced Thursday were his boldest move yet on trade, and a sign of resurgent power in the White House for economic adviser Peter Navarro and Commerce Secretary Wilbur L. Ross Jr., who have long pushed Mr. Trump to act more aggressively on trade, which was a signature campaign issue. They were a reminder to the Republican establishment that Mr. Trump's theory of the economy is sometimes at odds with traditional free-market conservatism, for as much as they overlap.

On Thursday, the conservative Wall Street Journal editorial board called the tariffs the "biggest policy blunder of his Presidency."

The move is also at odds with a broad and bipartisan swath of previous top White House economists, going back several administrations, who urged Mr. Trump in a letter last year "to avoid a policy that would likely incur greater economic and diplomatic costs than any conceivable national security gain." Jerome H. Powell, the new Federal Reserve chairman appointed by Mr. Trump, told Congress on Thursday that "the tariff approach is not the best approach" for trade disputes.

Mr. Trump, though, casts himself as protecting an industry he sees as endangered; raw steel production in America remains higher than it was 25 years ago, but it is down dramatically from the 1970s. As he tweeted on Friday:

**We must protect our country and our workers. Our steel industry is in bad shape. IF YOU DON'T HAVE STEEL, YOU DON'T HAVE A COUNTRY!**

**— Donald J. Trump (@realDonaldTrump) Mar 2, 2018**

Such rhetoric will likely boost Mr. Trump in industrial states such as Ohio and Pennsylvania, which were both key to his 2016 victory. But in the event of a trade war, they could rebound to hurt many of his other base voters. Last year, researchers at the Brookings Metropolitan Policy Program reported that small, rural communities would be disproportionately hurt by a trade shock.

They compiled a list of the 10 metro areas most vulnerable to such a shock because of their economic reliance on exports. Those areas were in Indiana, Texas, Louisiana, South Carolina and Alabama — all states Mr. Trump carried.

# Trump's Steel Tariffs Raise Fears of a Damaging Trade War

BY JIM TANKERSLEY | MARCH 2, 2018

WASHINGTON — After making good on tax cuts and regulatory rollbacks that business leaders wanted, President Trump has turned to a part of his economic agenda that many of them feared: tariffs.

Those leaders worry that Mr. Trump, by imposing stiff and sweeping tariffs on steel and aluminum, will set off a trade war with other countries. The global tit-for-tat could hurt American exporters and raise costs for manufacturers that rely on a vast supply chain around the world.

If that happens, it will crimp economic growth, undermining the stimulative effects of Mr. Trump's deregulation push and his signature $1.5 trillion tax cut.

The odds of such an outcome now appear to be rising, prompting congressional Republicans to push Mr. Trump in public and in private to reconsider. "If the president goes through with this, it will kill American jobs — that's what every trade war ultimately does," Senator Ben Sasse, Republican of Nebraska, said on Friday. "So much losing."

So far, Mr. Trump is not having any of that criticism, saying on Twitter on Friday that "trade wars are good, and easy to win."

That's not how trade wars usually go.

Even the prospect of a trade war could hurt the economic expansion underway. That's because any uncertainty can prompt companies to curtail investment or hold off on hiring.

If other countries follow up on their threats to retaliate, the pain could be significant. Beyond tariffs, their tools include taking strategic strikes at certain industries or taking their grievances to the World Trade Organization.

Any actions threaten the global supply chains on which the American economy is heavily dependent. The number of workers who will lose out if countries are cut off from America far exceeds the number who stand to gain from the pending tariffs.

"Industries that buy steel and aluminum, not to mention agricultural exporters, employ many times more people than the industries that the president wants to protect," said Peter A. Petri, an economist and trade expert at Brandeis University's International Business School. "Whether we go through with his approach is anyone's guess, but business investment depends on predictable policy, and relentless chaos takes its toll even if cooler heads prevail on the policies that the president is tweeting about."

Mr. Trump's planned tariffs would, in effect, levy a tax of 25 percent on imported steel and 10 percent on imported aluminum. The goal is to counter China, Russia and other countries that have flooded the global markets with cheap products and made it harder for the American steel industry to compete.

If put into effect, the tariffs would raise the price of steel and aluminum, squeezing automakers, beverage manufacturers and other industries that buy a lot of those materials. That would increase prices for consumers, kill some jobs in those industries or both.

The tariffs would almost certainly provoke a response from America's trading partners — and not just China and Russia, because they would apply to every other country. On Friday, the European Union threatened to retaliate by imposing tariffs of its own on some goods from America, including bluejeans, bourbon and motorcycles.

If the back-and-forth stopped there, the American economy would lose 0.1 percent of its output this year, said Mark Zandi, the chief economist at Moody's Analytics. That loss would cost the country 190,000 jobs.

What worries many economists is the prospect that the retaliation will go even further. A cycle of increasingly harsh tariffs would slam the brakes on global growth.

Here is one way the dispute could worsen: By provoking responses from Canada and Mexico, the tariffs could derail the current renegotiation of the North American Free Trade Agreement. Mr. Trump

Rolled steel being lifted into storage at a Nucor mill in Huger, S.C. Some economists see less potential for a trade war: "I don't think it will spiral out of control," said Thea M. Lee, president of the Economic Policy Institute.

could pull the United States out of that agreement, which would erect new and damaging trade barriers on agricultural exports from states such as Iowa.

Another possibility is that other countries could file complaints with the World Trade Organization. The W.T.O. could declare that the tariffs violated global trading rules, but the Trump administration, which has marginalized the organization, could choose to ignore it.

Such a move would stir chaos in the global trading regime. It would be like ejecting the referee from a playoff basketball game. A free-for-all could ensue, with countries levying tariffs or subsidizing domestic exporters in ways the W.T.O. would never allow.

Mr. Zandi estimates that a Nafta breakdown would cost the United States 1.8 million jobs. He calculates that a full global trade war, while far less likely, would carry much higher risks, including nearly four million lost American jobs.

"The economic fallout from such a war could be serious," he said, "ending in a global recession."

Others expressed less concern: In an era of globalization, the talk of retaliation may be stronger than the actual action. And some economists, particularly those on the left, even saw a possible bright side.

Jared Bernstein, an economist in the Obama administration who is now at the Center on Budget and Policy Priorities, expects some counter-tariffs, maybe from China on food products.

"You always hear trade war at these moments," Mr. Bernstein said. "That doesn't mean that's always wrong, but it usually is."

Thea M. Lee, a trade economist and the president of the Economic Policy Institute, a liberal think tank, said the tariffs could actually help global markets. They would punish countries that overproduce steel and aluminum, she said, and bring stability and certainty to producers of those metals in the United States.

"It's not actually in anybody's interest to spiral downward and get into a massive retaliatory situation," Ms. Lee said. "I think there will be some immediate reactions, but I don't think it will spiral out of control."

From the beginning of his insurgent 2016 presidential campaign, Mr. Trump has seen "winning" on trade as critical for the economy. Reducing trade deficits, he has argued, will work in tandem with lowering taxes and reducing federal regulations to supercharge growth. Mr. Trump took several steps last year to freeze or roll back regulations, and he signed a $1.5 trillion tax-cut bill in December. He also took initial steps to reorient trade policy, pulling out of the Trans-Pacific Partnership and embarking on the fractious renegotiation of Nafta.

While economic growth accelerated, the trade deficit in goods and services widened to $566 billion last year, the largest amount since 2008. The goods deficit with China hit $375 billion, a record.

The tariffs that Mr. Trump announced Thursday were his boldest move yet on trade. They were also a reminder to the Republican establishment that his theory of the economy is sometimes at odds with traditional free-market conservatism, despite much overlap.

On Thursday, the conservative Wall Street Journal editorial board called the tariffs the "biggest policy blunder of his presidency." The top two Republicans in Congress — the Senate majority leader, Mitch McConnell, and the House speaker, Paul D. Ryan — were imploring Mr. Trump privately to reconsider.

Mr. Trump, though, casts himself as protecting an industry that he sees as endangered. Raw steel production in America remains higher than it was 25 years ago, but it is down significantly from the 1970s. Just under 140,000 Americans work in the steel industry, according to the American Iron and Steel Institute.

While Mr. Trump's stand is likely to give him a boost in industrial states like Ohio and Pennsylvania, which were both key to his 2016 victory, a trade war may harm other manufacturing strongholds that are home to his base voters.

Last year, researchers at the Brookings Institution's Metropolitan Policy Program reported that smaller metropolitan areas would be disproportionately hurt by a trade shock. The 10 that were most vulnerable, because of their economic reliance on exports, were in Indiana, Texas, Louisiana, South Carolina and Alabama — all states Mr. Trump carried.

# What History Has to Say About the 'Winners' in Trade Wars

BY JAMES B. STEWART  |  MARCH 8, 2018

WITH PRESIDENT TRUMP ordering steep new tariffs on imported steel and aluminum on Thursday, and with America's trading partners threatening to retaliate, it looks as if Mr. Trump will get the trade war that he seems to want and that he thinks will be "easy" for the United States to win.

"Trade wars aren't so bad," he had said at the White House on Wednesday.

Which made me wonder: What trade wars does Mr. Trump have in mind?

The most prominent trade war of the 20th century was ignited by the Smoot-Hawley Tariff act of 1930, which imposed steep tariffs

LIBRARY OF CONGRESS

Senator Reed Smoot and Representative Willis C. Hawley at the U.S. Capitol in December 1929.

on roughly 20,000 imported goods. Led by Canada, America's trading partners retaliated with tariffs on United States exports, which plunged 61 percent from 1929 to 1933. The tariffs were repealed in 1934.

Historians and economists continue to debate the extent of the damage to the global economy, but there is little disagreement that Smoot-Hawley and the ensuing trade war exacerbated and prolonged the hardships of the Great Depression. Many historians contend it also contributed to the rise of the Nazis and other fascist parties. There is almost universal agreement that no one "won" that trade war.

Smoot-Hawley "was such a disaster that it's held sway over American trade policy for over 80 years," said Joshua Meltzer, a senior fellow at the Brookings Institution who also teaches international trade law at Johns Hopkins University. "No one wants to repeat it."

He called Mr. Trump's comments on trade wars "a dramatic departure" from economic orthodoxy.

On the question of who wins, "the easy answer is to say that no one wins a trade war," said Marc-William Palen, a professor of history at the University of Exeter in Britain and the author of "The 'Conspiracy' of Free Trade," which examines trade rivalry between the United States and the British Empire in the 19th century. "But the more I reflect on it, it seems the winners are those nations that don't take part."

Professor Palen cited the late-19th-century trade wars between Canada and the United States, which caused a precipitous drop in Canadian exports to America and led Canada to seek export markets in Britain. "The British Empire was the winner," he said.

Another "big winner" from a trade war it was not involved in, Professor Palen said, was Soviet Russia, which was largely shunned by Western trading partners after the 1917 revolution and the rise of communism, and was desperate for hard currency. The Smoot-Hawley tariffs, Professor Palen said, caused countries like Italy to abandon American imports and resume trading with the Soviets, forging trade links that persist today.

President Trump discussing foreign trade and steel production with corporate leaders at the White House this month. "Trade wars aren't so bad," Mr. Trump said this week.

A textbook case of one country's "winning" a trade war occurred during the late 19th century when a newly unified Italy imposed steep tariffs on imports from France in order to spur domestic industrialization. France, which was much richer and stronger, retaliated with tariffs against Italy, and Italian exports to France collapsed. Even after Italy abandoned its tariffs, France continued to punish Italy for years with high tariffs.

"France won in the sense that the trade war was brutal for the Italians," said John Conybeare, emeritus professor of political science at the University of Iowa, and the author of the book "Trade Wars."

Professor Conybeare said an enduring lesson from that trade conflict was that if there is a wide disparity in economic strength between two countries, the stronger country will probably prevail. "Trump must be thinking that the large size of the U.S. domestic market gives it a lot of bargaining power in any trade dispute," he said.

While that may be true with much smaller, weaker countries, it is not the case with trading partners of equal or even larger size, such as the European Union and China. "Without that large disparity in economic strength, both sides lose," Professor Conybeare said.

He cited what have become known as the "chicken wars" of the early 1960s, a trade dispute set off when Germany and France imposed tariffs on American chicken. The United States retaliated by imposing tariffs on an array of goods, including French brandy, light trucks and Volkswagen buses. The United States even threatened to reduce its troop presence in Europe. Despite those pressures, the newly formed European Economic Community did not back down, and in that sense the United States "lost" the war.

The biggest losers, though, were American and European consumers deprived of choices in the marketplace and forced to pay higher prices for what was available.

There were also unintended consequences. American automakers, insulated from foreign competition by the tariffs, failed to modernize, improve quality or reduce costs, setting the stage for a decades-long decline, which for Chrysler and General Motors ended in bankruptcy.

Much the same can be said of the United States steel industry, which since World War II has probably received more protection from tariffs and quotas than any other industry. "They just used the protection to raise prices, fatten profits, pay their executives more and avoid automating and reducing costs," Professor Conybeare said. "They didn't use the breathing space they gained to modernize. So much of the U.S. steel industry is using obsolete technology, which is why they can't compete."

Decades of tariff protection have done little to stem the industry's decline. Domestic steel employment dropped from 135,000 in 2000 to 83,600 in 2016, according to the Bureau of Labor Statistics.

Much like Mr. Trump, President George W. Bush veered from Republican free trade orthodoxy in 2002 when he imposed tariffs of up to 30 percent on certain steel products to counter what he claimed was a surge of imports (Canada, Mexico and a number of developing countries were exempted). Although the tariffs were loudly condemned by many Republicans, politicians from steel-producing states supported the move and protectionist Democrats like Representative Richard Gephardt of Missouri argued that the measures did not go far enough.

The European Union filed charges with the World Trade Organization, which ruled that the tariffs were illegal and discriminatory and authorized up to $2 billion in retaliatory measures. The E.U. threatened tariffs on a variety of American products, including autos and Florida oranges.

Mr. Bush abandoned the tariffs in December 2003. He claimed that they had served their purpose, but subsequent studies suggested that they had little impact on employment in the industry and led to a loss of hundreds of thousands of jobs in industries that use steel as a raw material.

Mr. Trump's pronouncements on trade this week "sound like a very archaic, 19th-century argument," Professor Palen said, referring to a time when protectionism was Republican orthodoxy and Representative William McKinley of Ohio, who later became president, was successfully promoting his Tariff Act of 1890, which raised the average duty on imports to nearly 50 percent.

The act is widely considered by historians to have been a disaster that led to higher consumer prices and inflation and provoked a voter backlash. Republicans lost their House majority in 1890 and lost the White House and both houses of Congress in 1892. The act was repealed in 1894.

In any trade war, as that example suggests, "the big losers are consumers, who are the vast majority of people," Professor Palen said. "A few industries may benefit, but there are way more losers than winners. And the poor are the biggest losers of all. People like Trump may not care that much about paying a few extra dollars. But a lot of people don't have that luxury."

# Trump Tariffs Threaten National Security

OPINION | BY JENNIFER A. HILLMAN | JUNE 1, 2018

THE TRUMP ADMINISTRATION has made three reckless moves on trade in recent days. On May 23, it launched an investigation into whether imports of cars and S.U.V.s threaten the national security of the United States. Then President Trump signaled that he'd let Chinese telecommunications giant ZTE off the hook, despite its "false statements" and repeated violations of United States sanctions on North Korea or Iran. Thursday brought a third misguided decision to impose tariffs on steel and aluminum from our staunchest allies, including Canada and the European Union, again contending that their exports threaten our national security.

"Economic security is military security," Commerce Secretary Wilbur Ross has said. But this administration's push to blur, or even erase, the line between our economic and national security interests is dangerous — both for the United States and for the world.

First, the Trump administration is making overly broad interpretations of national security and then insisting these claims cannot be challenged. These actions undermine international law and threaten the rules-based global trading system.

The law being invoked to justify these new tariffs was crafted during the Cold War. It gives the president broad power to ensure that the United States is not overly dependent on imports for critical defense needs, especially imports from countries we don't trust to supply us in times of war.

International law is more precise. It allows countries to pile on tariffs or take other actions that would otherwise violate their trade commitments when they judge them necessary to protect their essential security interests. This exception applies only in cases related to trade in nuclear materials, arms or ammunition; or during war or international emergency. Mr. Trump's tariffs do not fit within any of those boxes.

Those who crafted the "national security" exception to the international trading rules tried to balance every country's need to judge their own national security risks with the concern that an open-ended exception would be misused. Hence, "national security" is limited to cases involving emergencies, war and weapons. The Trump administration has upset that balance. If the United States can justify tariffs on cars as a threat to national security, then every country in the world can most likely justify restrictions on almost any product under a similar claim.

For more than two decades after the World Trade Organization was created in 1995, no claim for breaking the trade rules through the national security exception had ever reached a W.T.O. dispute settlement panel. None of the member countries wanted to allow the "nameless, faceless" bureaucrats in Geneva to define their essential security interests.

That changed in 2017, with a claim by Russia, which had imposed myriad trade and transit restrictions on Ukraine, which challenged the Russian measures at the W.T.O. In the dispute, Russia contends that the moment any country claims its actions are based on national security, the judges hearing the case must put down their pens and go home. The only W.T.O. member joining Russia's contention is the United States.

This is dangerous. It provides all countries with a "get out of jail free" card that can be played just by saying the magic words "national security."

Blurring the line between economic and national security also invites retaliation. The United States agreed to eliminate steel tariffs and lower aluminum tariffs to below 5 percent in 1995 in exchange for tariff cuts by others. Now, by imposing 25 percent tariffs on steel and 10 percent on aluminum, the United States has broken that commitment. And by imposing the tariffs on some but not all trading partners (South Korea, Australia, Argentina and Brazil are exempt), the United States has also broken its commitment not to discriminate among W.T.O. members.

Already our partners are reacting. China has placed tariffs on American exports of nuts, fruits, wine, pork and some steel pipes. Canada, the European Union, Mexico, Japan, India, Turkey and Russia may impose their own retaliatory tariffs. This adds tremendous chaos to the trading system and may signal the start of a global trade war.

Moreover, the Trump administration is sacrificing real national security concerns for short-term economic gains. How else to describe a decision to dispose of the Commerce Department's settlement with ZTE? It followed a multiyear investigation finding 380 alleged and admitted violations of American law by the Chinese telecomm giant. These included conspiracies, false statements and deceptions to obtain contracts to supply, build, and operate telecommunications networks in Iran, and to illegally ship telecommunications equipment to North Korea.

If we impose tariffs on steel and cars based on a claim that those imports threaten our national security, what will we do if and when our national security is really threatened? Auto production in the United States has more than doubled since 2009, and imports of Chinese steel have fallen by nearly 75 percent since their 2014 peak. Why attack imports from longstanding allies now? Especially when it does nothing to target China's massive subsidies, intellectual property theft, and unfair takeovers of technology — actions that truly threaten our national security.

Erasing the line dividing national security from economic security threatens both. Congress needs to recognize the danger and limit the president's authority to raise the specter of national security at every turn. At the same time, Congress must ensure that genuine concerns are not traded away for limited economic gains. Cavalier use of rarely invoked laws will only undermine their purpose and put the trading system at risk.

**JENNIFER A. HILLMAN** is a professor at Georgetown University Law Center and was a member of the World Trade Organization's Appellate Body from 2007-11.

# Senators Ask White House Economists to Turn Over Tariff Findings

BY ALAN RAPPEPORT | JUNE 14, 2018

WASHINGTON — Two senators have asked President Trump's Council of Economic Advisers to turn over an analysis that shows the administration's tariffs would slow economic growth.

The internal analysis, which was first reported by The New York Times last week, contradicts the public statements of several Trump administration officials who have said that Mr. Trump's plan to impose tariffs on aluminum, steel and a broad array of Chinese products will not dampen economic growth. The existence of such a study has raised questions about whether the Trump administration

DOUG MILLS/THE NEW YORK TIMES

Two senators have asked Kevin Hassett, the chairman of the Council of Economic Advisers, to hand over an internal analysis showing how tariffs could hurt economic growth.

is pursuing policies that its own experts know is at odds with economic reality.

Senator Ron Johnson, a Republican from Wisconsin, and Senator Claire McCaskill, a Democrat from Missouri, sent a letter to Kevin Hassett, chairman of the council, asking him to hand over any research on tariffs by June 27. The two senators, who sent the letter on Wednesday, lead the Committee on Homeland Security and Governmental Affairs.

"To better understand the potential consequences of the administration's trade policies, we respectfully request that you produce the C.E.A. economic analysis relating to the administration's steel and aluminum tariffs and all supporting data and documents," they wrote.

The council does not publicly release all of its research and it is not clear how much damage it estimates the tariffs and potential retaliation from other countries would do to the administration's economic growth projections. Mr. Trump has made achieving sustainable 3 percent economic growth a centerpiece of his agenda.

Mr. Hassett has dodged the question when asked about it in public settings, suggesting that the threat of tariffs will encourage other countries to lower their trade barriers and therefore boost global economic growth.

"If you model a future where everybody else reduces their trade barriers to ours, then that's massively good for the global economy and massively good for the U.S. economy," Mr. Hassett said last week.

Gary D. Cohn, the former director of Mr. Trump's National Economic Council, said at an event hosted by The Washington Post on Thursday that he was already seeing signs that companies were holding back on investment out of fears of a trade war. He said that tit-for-tat tariffs could negate the economic benefits of Mr. Trump's tax cuts.

"If you end up with a tariff battle, you will end up with price inflation, you could end up with more consumer debt, those are all historic ingredients for an economic slowdown," Mr. Cohn said.

On Wednesday, Federal Reserve Chairman Jerome H. Powell acknowledged anecdotal concern about business investment slowing as a result of the tariffs but said, so far, the Fed had no data to support that.

"We really don't see it in the numbers," he said. "I would put it down as more of a risk."

A C.E.A. spokeswoman did not immediately respond to a request for comment about the Senate request.

# U.S. and China Expand Trade War as Beijing Matches Trump's Tariffs

BY ANA SWANSON | JUNE 15, 2018

WASHINGTON — The Trump administration on Friday escalated a trade war between the world's two largest economies, moving ahead with tariffs on $50 billion of Chinese goods and provoking an immediate tit-for-tat response from Beijing.

The president is battling on a global front, taking aim at allies and adversaries alike. The United States has levied global tariffs on metal imports that include those from Europe, Canada and Mexico, while threatening to tear up the North American Free Trade Agreement.

These countries are fighting back, drawing up retaliatory measures that go after products in Mr. Trump's political base. China's response was swift on Friday, focusing on $50 billion worth of American goods including beef, poultry, tobacco and cars.

The trade actions could ripple through the global economy, fracturing supply chains and costing jobs at American companies that will be forced to absorb higher prices. Although the United States economy is especially strong, the tariffs are expected to drive up prices for American consumers as well as for businesses that depend on China for parts.

Things could get worse if the United States and China ratchet up their actions. Mr. Trump has already promised more tariffs in response to China's retaliation. China, in turn, is likely to back away from an agreement to buy $70 billion worth of American agricultural and energy products — a deal that was conditional on the United States lifting its threat of tariffs.

"China's proportionate and targeted tariffs on U.S. imports are meant to send a strong signal that it will not capitulate to U.S. demands," said Eswar Prasad, a professor of international trade at

Employees at a manufacturing plant in McKeesport, Pa., earlier this year. China said it will hit back by imposing its own tariffs on United States goods.

Cornell University. "It will be challenging for both sides to find a way to de-escalate these tensions."

The penalties make good on a campaign promise by Mr. Trump to crack down on Chinese trade practices that he says have cost American jobs. On Friday, Mr. Trump said in a statement that trade between the countries had been "very unfair, for a very long time."

Mr. Trump added, "These tariffs are essential to preventing further unfair transfers of American technology and intellectual property to China, which will protect American jobs."

But the White House has lately vacillated between taking a tough stance on Chinese trade practices and declaring that the trade war was "on hold."

In recent weeks, the administration had tried to defuse tensions with China ahead of a summit meeting with the North Korean leader.

Mr. Trump extended a lifeline to the Chinese telecommunications company, ZTE, at the request of President Xi Jinping.

Some advisers, including the treasury secretary, Steven Mnuchin, had feared the economic consequences of a trade war and pushed for a negotiated solution instead. The latest action appears to be a victory for the more hard-line faction of the Trump administration, including the president's trade advisers, Robert E. Lighthizer and Peter Navarro, who have pushed for a protectionist approach.

"This is not about a policy," said Mickey Kantor, the former commerce secretary and a chief trade negotiator for the Clinton administration. "This is not about asserting U.S. leadership. It's about the president having an impulse that if he does this, he will strengthen his base, send a signal to China, and be able to say he's been strong and tough."

Tariffs of 25 percent on roughly $34 billion of Chinese products — drawn from a list that the administration published in April that has since been refined — will go into effect on July 6, the office of the United States trade representative said. The administration is also proposing tariffs on roughly $16 billion of new products, which it said would undergo further review, including public hearings.

In total, the tariffs will fall on 1,102 categories of Chinese goods, including nuclear reactors, aircraft engine parts, bulldozers, ball bearings, motorcycles and industrial and agricultural machinery. The list generally focuses on industrial sectors that relate to the country's Made in China 2025 plan for dominating high-tech industries, like aerospace, automobiles, information technology and robotics, the administration said.

The revised list dropped some products purchased directly by American consumers, including flat-screen televisions and printer accessories, while adding semiconductors, machinery and plastics, according to an analysis by Chad Bown, a senior fellow at the Peterson Institute for International Economics.

In a call with reporters Friday, a senior official said the administration would soon roll out a process for companies to apply for exclusions to the tariffs for products they cannot get from another source.

China said it would hit back with additional tariffs of 25 percent on about $50 billion of American-made products, the country's Commerce Ministry said in a release. These will also come in two rounds, with penalties on about $34 billion of goods, including agricultural products, automobiles and seafood, scheduled to take effect the same day as the United States tariffs. Tariffs on another $16 billion worth of American goods, including medical equipment, chemical products and energy products, will be announced later, the ministry said.

The ministry said in a separate statement Friday that all other recent trade terms negotiated by the United States and China would also be declared invalid.

Tensions could escalate further in the coming weeks. The White House is formulating a plan for restricting Chinese investments in the United States and putting stricter limitations on the types of advanced technology that can be exported to the country. It has said those restrictions will go into effect shortly after they are announced by June 30.

The White House says its measures are necessary to reset the trade relationship with China, a country Trump administration officials accuse of manipulating economic rules and costing millions of American jobs.

The moves could damp economic growth that has been stoked by the administration's tax cuts — though the overall effects are likely to be limited because of the small size of the tariffs relative to the American economy. But in a few industries that are heavily affected, the pain could be substantial. Economists say the tariffs will drive up prices for American consumers purchasing products at retail stores as well as for businesses that depend on China for parts used to make other goods in the United States.

Goldman Sachs economists said Friday that the initial tariffs on $34 billion of products would have a minimal effect on growth and inflation, in part because it was concentrated on industrial rather than consumer goods. But they cautioned that the president's moves raised the odds that other measures, including more tariffs from the United States and China and restrictions on investment, would follow.

In another analysis, the Tax Foundation, a conservative nonprofit organization, found that tariffs on China and steel and aluminum would have a minimal impact on growth and wages, but that it could lower American employment by more than 45,000 full-time jobs in the long run.

"Imposing tariffs places the cost of China's unfair trade practices squarely on the shoulders of American consumers, manufacturers, farmers and ranchers," said Thomas J. Donohue, the president of the United States Chamber of Commerce. "This is not the right approach."

The National Retail Federation, which represents grocers, chain restaurants and other stores, said the tariffs would not combat China's abusive trade practices, but only "strain the budgets of working families by raising consumer prices."

But the tariffs received commendation from others, including lawmakers across the political spectrum who have urged the president to remain tough on China. Senator Marco Rubio, Republican of Florida, called the announcement an "excellent move," while Senator Chuck Schumer of New York, the Democratic leader, said the tariffs were "right on target."

"China is our real trade enemy, and their theft of intellectual property and their refusal to let our companies compete fairly threatens millions of future American jobs," Mr. Schumer said.

CAO LI contributed reporting from Hong Kong. ELSIE CHEN in Beijing and HIROKO TABUCHI also contributed research and translation.

# Trump's 'Bully' Attack on Trudeau Outrages Canadians

BY DAN BILEFSKY AND CATHERINE PORTER | JUNE 10, 2018

MONTREAL — Canadians have had enough.

It takes a lot to rile people in this decidedly courteous nation. But after President Trump's parting shots against Prime Minister Justin Trudeau on the day he left the Group of 7 summit meeting in Quebec, the country reacted with uncharacteristic outrage and defiance at a best friend's nastiness.

"It was extremely undiplomatic and antagonistic," Frank McKenna, a former Canadian ambassador to the United States, wrote in an email. "It was disrespectful and ill informed."

"All Canadians will support the prime minister in standing up to this bully," he added. "Friends do not treat friends with such contempt."

Even Mr. Trudeau's political foes rose to his defense.

"We will stand shoulder to shoulder with the prime minister and the people of Canada," Doug Ford, the Trump-like renegade who was recently elected premier of Ontario, wrote on Twitter.

Stephen Harper, the former Conservative prime minister whom Mr. Trudeau beat to become prime minister, told Fox News on Sunday that Mr. Trump had made a mistake targeting trade relations with Canada.

"I can understand why President Trump, why the American people feel they need some better trade relationships," he said. But, he added, "this is the wrong target."

The ink had barely dried on the communiqué after the G-7 summit meeting in Charlevoix, Quebec, when President Trump berated Mr. Trudeau on Twitter from Air Force One, accusing him of being "very dishonest and weak" and of making up "false statements."

"Based on Justin's false statements at his news conference, and the fact that Canada is charging massive Tariffs to our U.S. farmers, workers and companies, I have instructed our U.S. Reps not to endorse the Communique as we look at Tariffs on automobiles flooding the U.S. Market!" Mr. Trump wrote.

As Canadians were recovering from the sting of those remarks, Mr. Trump's economic adviser Larry Kudlow piled on, saying on television that Mr. Trudeau had "stabbed us in the back," betrayed Mr. Trump and made him look weak before his summit meeting on Tuesday with North Korea's leader.

And Peter Navarro, the president's top trade adviser, suggested on Fox News Sunday that "there's a special place in hell" for Mr. Trudeau.

Mr. Trump's ire appears to have been spurred after Mr. Trudeau said Canada would retaliate against United States tariffs on steel and aluminum products, calling them "kind of insulting" and saying that Canadians "are nice" but "we will not be pushed around."

These were strong words from the telegenic, soft-spoken leader, who has spent the two-day summit trying to strike a precarious balance between being Canada's protector-in-chief but not inciting the mercurial American president. But Canadian officials said they were perplexed by Mr. Trump's reaction since nothing Mr. Trudeau said was new.

From Singapore, where he is scheduled to meet with Kim Jong-un of North Korea for a historic summit, Mr. Trump again took to Twitter on Monday to assail Mr. Trudeau.

"Fair Trade is now to be called Fool Trade if it is not Reciprocal. According to a Canada release, they make almost 100 Billion Dollars in Trade with U.S. (guess they were bragging and got caught!)," Mr. Trump wrote. "Minimum is 17B. Tax Dairy from us at 270%. Then Justin acts hurt when called out!"

Mr. Trump is not exactly popular in Canada. And the Twitter tirade threatened to inflame already boiling resentment of the president, whose anti-immigrant stances and skepticism of climate change have infuriated many in a country that prides itself on its openness and social responsibility.

A Pew Research survey published last year found that Canadian antagonism toward Mr. Trump had helped reduce Canadians' opinions of the United States to a low not seen in more than three decades, with only 43 percent of Canadians holding a favorable view of the country.

Canadians across the political spectrum said that while the world had grown used to Mr. Trump's social media rants, the ferocity and personal tone of the insults against Mr. Trudeau had crossed a line. Some even asked whether Canadians should boycott United States products and stop traveling south of the border.

Canada's foreign minister, Chrystia Freeland, told reporters that Canadians should be insulted by Mr. Trump's tariffs on steel and aluminum, imposed because, the president said, Canada poses a national security threat to the United States.

"The national security pretext is absurd and frankly insulting to Canadians, the closest and strongest ally the United States has had," Ms. Freeland said.

As to the biting comments made by Mr. Kudlow, she responded, "Canada does not believe that ad hominem attacks are a particularly appropriate or useful way to conduct our relations with other countries."

She added, "We particularly refrain from ad hominem attacks when it comes to our allies."

Ms. Freeland said she planned to continue negotiating with the Americans over trade. "We are always prepared to talk," she said. "That's the Canadian way: always ready to talk and always absolutely clear about standing up for Canada."

But for now, calling the American tariffs illegal and unjustified, she reiterated Canada's intention to impose retaliatory tariffs, starting July 1, "which is Canada Day," she noted. "Perhaps not inappropriate."

For Mr. Trudeau, the G-7 summit meeting has been an important test of his leadership, at home and on the global stage. On Sunday, he continued his schedule, meeting with world leaders and trying to rise above the Twitter insults from his neighbor.

He wrote on Twitter on Sunday that the agreement at Charlevoix would, among other things, strengthen "our economies," and protect women and the environment. "That's what matters."

Canadian fury at Trump notwithstanding, analysts said it was difficult to overstate the damage that bad relations with him could cause to the Canadian economy. Canada relies on the United States as its only neighbor, its military ally and its largest trading partner.

About 1.9 million Canadian jobs are tied directly to trade with the United States, which absorbs almost three-quarters of Canada's exports.

"Any Canadian prime minister, no matter what the American president does or says, has to deal with the president of the United States," said Janice Stein, founding director of the University of Toronto's Munk School of Global Affairs.

Nevertheless, some analysts said Mr. Trump's attack could work to politically embolden Mr. Trudeau, a Liberal, whose popularity has been waning here after a series of missteps and the rise of populism, including Mr. Ford's recent election as the premier of Ontario.

John J. Kirton, director of the G-7 Research Group at the University of Toronto, a network of people who study the gatherings, said Mr. Trudeau, who faces an election next year, needed to appeal to rural voters in Ontario and Quebec and show he was protecting Canada's heartland in the face of Mr. Trump's protectionism.

"Every Canadian prime minister has to be seen to protect the dairy sector," Mr. Kirton said. Mr. Trump has repeatedly attacked Canada's tariffs on dairy imports.

Mr. Trudeau has been philosophical about the limits of Canada's ability to placate Mr. Trump.

"If the expectation was that a weekend in beautiful Charlevoix, surrounded by all sorts of lovely people, was going to transform the president's outlook on trade and the world," he said in his final news conference at the summit meeting before the tweet storm, "then we didn't quite perhaps meet that bar."

# Escalating Clash With Canada, Trump Is Isolated Before North Korea Meeting

BY PETER BAKER | JUNE 10, 2018

WASHINGTON — President Trump escalated a bitter clash with some of America's closest allies on Sunday, lashing out through his advisers at Canada's prime minister in unusually personal terms and leaving himself with a diplomatic crisis as he arrived in Asia to negotiate a nuclear agreement with North Korea.

A day after Mr. Trump refused to sign a communiqué of the Group of 7 major industrial economies, he and his advisers went on the attack, accusing Prime Minister Justin Trudeau of "betrayal" and a "stab" in the back, even as Canada, Germany and France pushed back against what they called the American president's "insult" and "inconsistency."

The exchange left Mr. Trump estranged from America's partners at the very moment he is about to stride onto the most important world stage he has assumed since taking office. Aides attributed his outburst over the weekend to his feeling undercut as he prepared to meet with the North Korean leader, Kim Jong-un, while critics said he had stiff-armed his friends at the expense of a unified front.

Whether Mr. Kim sees Mr. Trump's combative approach as a sign of strength or weakness, the rupture with other major powers was sure to shadow the session between the two in Singapore on Tuesday, the first time leaders of the United States and North Korea will have met in person. Mr. Trump's strategy for pressuring Mr. Kim to give up his nuclear weapons has depended on isolating North Korea, but he arrived in Singapore looking isolated himself.

"I've never seen anything like this," said Robert D. Hormats, who advised Republican and Democratic presidents at a dozen Group of 7 summit meetings, starting at the first in Rambouillet, France, in 1975, when it was still the Group of 6.

"The irony is this institution that was designed largely by the United States was really designed to shore up alliances and political relationships and resolve economic issues. This just served to do the opposite of that."

The latest meeting, held in Canada, was tense amid disputes over trade, security and other issues. But after negotiators for all seven countries crafted a final communiqué that even the reluctant American delegation agreed to, Mr. Trump abruptly lashed out on Twitter from Air Force One on Saturday night.

He refused to sign the communiqué, saying Mr. Trudeau had made "false statements" at an end-of-summit news conference, and calling the Canadian leader "dishonest & weak."

By Sunday morning, Mr. Trump's aides were adding fire to the attack on Mr. Trudeau. Larry Kudlow, the president's economic adviser, said that Mr. Trudeau's comments were "a betrayal" and that he had "stabbed us in the back." Mr. Trump "is not going to let a Canadian prime minister push him around," Mr. Kudlow said on CNN's "State of the Union" program, adding, "He is not going to permit any show of weakness on the trip to negotiate with North Korea."

Peter Navarro, the president's trade adviser, was even harsher. "There's a special place in hell for any foreign leader that engages in bad-faith diplomacy with President Donald J. Trump and then tries to stab him in the back on the way out the door," Mr. Navarro said on "Fox News Sunday."

Mr. Trump finally weighed in again on Sunday night with a cascade of fresh tweets targeting Canada, Germany and the European Union, accusing them of unfair trade practices and of not spending enough on their security. He cited a series of selective statistics about Canadian-American trade, adding derisively, "Then Justin acts hurt when called out!"

Left unclear was what exactly Mr. Trudeau had said that so offended Mr. Trump. During his Saturday news conference, the prime minister was relatively measured but repeated his position that Canada "will not be pushed around" and would respond to American tariffs with tariffs of its own.

Mr. Trudeau on Sunday publicly ignored the dispute, instead hailing "the historic and important agreement" that "will help make our economies stronger & people more prosperous," as he wrote on Twitter.

But his foreign minister, Chrystia Freeland, told reporters that if anyone should be insulted, it was Canada, because Mr. Trump had cited a national security justification for his tariffs on steel and aluminum. "The national security pretext is absurd and frankly insulting to Canadians, the closest and strongest ally the United States has had," she said. "That is where the insult lies."

As for the comments by Mr. Trump's aides, she said, "Canada does not believe that ad hominem attacks are a particularly appropriate or useful way to conduct our relations with other countries."

Roland Paris, a former foreign affairs adviser to Mr. Trudeau, went further. "Big tough guy once he's back on his airplane," he wrote on Twitter. "Can't do it in person, and knows it, which makes him feel week. So he projects these feelings onto Trudeau and then lashes out at him. You don't need to be Freud. He's a pathetic little man-child."

Other members of the Group of 7 stood with Canada against Mr. Trump.

"International cooperation can't depend on anger and small words," France's Élysée Palace said in a statement. "Let's be serious and worthy of our people. We spent two days obtaining a draft and commitments. We stick to it. And anyone who leaves and turns their back on them shows their inconsistency."

Prime Minister Theresa May of Britain issued a statement through an aide saying she was "fully supportive of Justin Trudeau." The German foreign minister, Heiko Maas, on Sunday called on European nations to stick together following Mr. Trump's announcement.

"It's actually not a real surprise," Mr. Maas told reporters in Berlin. "We have seen this with the climate agreement or the Iran deal. In a matter of seconds, you can destroy trust with 280 Twitter characters. To build that up again will take much longer."

Mr. Trump never really wanted to attend the Group of 7 meeting, but aides pressed him to go even as they feared it would be a disaster because he was being forced to do something he did not want to do. He rebelled by showing up late and leaving early.

During closed-door meetings, Mr. Trump largely listened through most issues, firmly crossing his arms and swiveling a bit in his seat, according to people who were in the room. At points, he looked around trying to catch the eyes of others, as if looking for reassurance, the witnesses said. Some smiled back; others did not.

He arrived 18 minutes late for a Saturday session on gender equality and did not bother putting his headphones on for translation when President Emmanuel Macron of France spoke. At some points, Mr. Trump closed his eyes in what people in the room took to mean he was dozing off.

But he came alive whenever trade was mentioned, mocking and insulting other leaders, particularly Mr. Trudeau, Mr. Macron and Chancellor Angela Merkel of Germany, according to the witnesses. Ms. Merkel was clearly not happy but largely kept quiet, evidently not wanting to provoke more conflict. Mr. Trump's conversation was described by European officials as stream of consciousness, filled with superlatives but not following a linear argument.

Negotiators worked late Friday night to craft a statement that all seven leaders could sign. Mr. Trump's delegation objected to the term "rules-based international order" until negotiators compromised by expressing support for "a" rules-based order rather than "the" rules-based order.

In a section on trade, the Americans insisted on using the word "reciprocal," one of Mr. Trump's favorite terms. They compromised by expressing support for "creating reciprocal benefits." They did not refer directly to the Iran nuclear agreement, which Mr. Trump just pulled out of, but the Europeans included a reference to the United Nations Security Council resolution that endorsed the deal.

The negotiators included agree-to-disagree language on climate change and on an international commitment to reduce plastics in the world. And then the statement was released on Saturday night, only to have Mr. Trump disavow it. Mrs. May learned only as her helicopter arrived at the airport for her to board her plane to return to London.

"It started out as a good summit because we were actually talking to each other, instead of past each other," said Peter Beyer, the German government's coordinator on trans-Atlantic relations. But he added, "It looks like the U.S. is no longer a reliable partner in international agreements, and that's bad."

Josef Braml of the German Council on Foreign Relations said Mr. Trump considered diplomacy a waste of time. "He is about to destroy what's left of the liberal world order because he thinks rules and institutions help America's rivals, China and Europe," he said.

Laurence Nardon, director of the North American program at the French Institute of International Relations in Paris, said Mr. Trump's behavior was a negotiation trick. "It's like when a person leaves the room and slams the door, but is hoping the other person will run after them and follow them into the corridor," she said.

In Washington, Democrats and some Republicans were upset at the outcome. But Mr. Trump received support from a few Republicans who cheered his tough stance.

Representative Peter T. King, Republican of New York, called the episode a "warning shot to Kim Jong-un" in keeping with Mr. Trump's approach to negotiations. "This is the Trump style of getting things done," he said. As to the wisdom of such a public clash, he said, "It depends on how it turns out. This president lives on a high wire, and so far it's been working."

# Trump Expected to List China Tariffs, Potentially Reigniting Trade War

BY ALAN RAPPEPORT AND ANA SWANSON | JUNE 14, 2018

WASHINGTON — The White House is expected on Friday to release a final list of Chinese goods that it plans to subject to tariffs and could soon begin putting some of those levies into effect, potentially reigniting a trade war that had been on the back burner while President Trump engaged in delicate nuclear diplomacy with North Korea.

The Trump administration has vacillated between threatening tariffs on China and putting the trade war "on hold" as it tries to negotiate a deal with Beijing that would give American companies greater access to the Chinese market. Those negotiations have produced little in the way of a firm commitment, however, with China offering to purchase nearly $70 billion in energy, agricultural and manufactured products from the United States, but only if the White House suspends tariffs on Chinese products.

So far, the White House has given no indication that it plans to back away from its threat of tariffs, which President Trump and his advisers see as giving the United States leverage in negotiations with Beijing. But while the administration is expected to detail on Friday the final list of goods that it plans to subject to the tariffs, it may phase those in to allow for continuing discussions, according to people familiar with the administration's plans.

In early April, the Trump administration outlined a preliminary list of roughly $50 billion in Chinese products that would be subject to 25 percent tariffs — including televisions, medical devices, aircraft parts and batteries. It has since refined the list based on feedback from business owners, trade groups and other industry representatives, who testified at public hearings in Washington in mid-May.

Still, any plan to impose tariffs — even on just a subset of Chinese products — could restart a trade war between the world's two largest economies. China has threatened its own retaliatory tariffs on American goods, including soybeans, pork and steel. Mr. Trump responded by saying his administration would consider levies on another $100 billion in Chinese products, though that list has not been finalized or released publicly.

Sarah Huckabee Sanders, the White House press secretary, said on Thursday that the president's trade team had met to discuss the China tariffs, but she would not confirm when the list would be released or when the tariffs would go into effect. The White House has previously said that its levies will go into effect shortly after a list of affected products is published by June 15, and that restrictions on Chinese investment in the United States will follow.

Trump administration officials have been engaged in vigorous internal debates in recent weeks over how to proceed with China. Steven Mnuchin, the Treasury secretary, and Larry Kudlow, the director of the National Economic Council, have been pushing for a more modest agreement that satisfies Mr. Trump's desire to reduce the trade deficit. Peter Navarro, Mr. Trump's trade adviser, and Robert E. Lighthizer, the United States trade representative, have urged deeper structural reforms to China's industrial policy.

But negotiations with China have been complicated by Mr. Trump's diplomatic dance with North Korea, given the involvement of the Chinese president, Xi Jinping, in helping facilitate the nuclear talks. Some observers said the fact that the talks with North Korea appeared to have gone well might give Mr. Trump more leeway to punish China now.

"Key administration officials reportedly have reached a consensus that some sort of penalties are now justified, given the lack of progress in negotiations, and that China is unlikely to derail the ongoing process on North Korea because it is so consistent with their security interests," said Scott Kennedy, a China expert at the Center for Strategic and International Studies.

Mr. Trump has tried to remain unpredictable in the negotiations with China, ordering up to $150 billion in proposed tariffs and calling on the Treasury Department to develop a plan for restrictions on Chinese investment in the United States.

However, Mr. Trump has also offered concessions. He directed his Commerce Department to offer a lifeline to ZTE, the Chinese telecommunications company that was on the brink of shutting down, the result of harsh penalties for violating American sanctions. At the request of Mr. Xi, the Commerce Department agreed to a settlement with ZTE that included a $1 billion fine and the installation of a new compliance team.

Business groups have protested that tariffs on products from China would disrupt their supply chains, and that retaliation from Beijing could put valuable markets at risk.

"Tariffs are the wrong answer to China's ongoing discriminatory and damaging trade practices," said Dean Garfield, the president of the Information Technology Industry Council, which represents some of the country's largest tech firms. "By imposing tariffs on consumer goods and key components of such goods, the president would needlessly take money out of Americans' pockets — harming the very people he hopes to help, not punishing China."

No formal trade meetings between the United States and China are currently scheduled, but talks have continued to take place.

Mike Pompeo, the secretary of state, met on Thursday in Beijing with Wang Yi, China's foreign minister, to discuss the situation with North Korea, and he said that they also spoke about trade.

"Our deficit with China is still too high," Mr. Pompeo said. "I stressed how important it is for President Trump to rectify that situation so that trade becomes more balanced, more reciprocal and more fair, with the opportunity to have American workers be treated fairly."

In an interview on Fox News that was broadcast on Wednesday evening, Mr. Trump suggested that China had loosened its border with North Korea because it was frustrated with how strongly he is clamping down on trade. Mr. Trump said that within the next two weeks his hawkish approach to dealing with China on trade would be evident.

"They understand what we are doing," Mr. Trump said.

But fanning the trade dispute with China comes with big risks, given that the United States is waging separate trade fights with Europe, Canada and Mexico over its imposition of tariffs on foreign steel and aluminum. Those countries have threatened to retaliate with tariffs of their own, and Mexico is already hitting $3 billion worth of American products with tariffs.

On Thursday, the European Union's 28 member states unanimously endorsed a plan to impose import duties on 2.8 billion euros' worth of American products, according to Kinga Malinowska, a spokeswoman for the office of the European commissioner for trade, Cecilia Malmstrom.

Canada is prepared to put retaliatory tariffs on an array of American products on July 1 if the United States does not back down from its metals tariffs.

On Thursday, Chrystia Freeland, Canada's foreign minister, met with Mr. Lighthizer to discuss the future of the North American Free Trade Agreement, which is in doubt given disagreements between the United States and Canada and Mexico.

At a speech on Wednesday evening, Ms. Freeland offered a stark rebuke of America's protectionist trade policy and said that Mr. Trump's tariffs were "a naked example of the United States' putting its thumb on the scale, in violation of the very rules it helped to write."

**MILAN SCHREUER** contributed reporting from Brussels.

# United States and Mexico Are Nearing Nafta Compromise

BY ANA SWANSON  |  AUG. 3, 2018

WASHINGTON — The United States and Mexico are edging closer to agreement on how to rewrite key portions of the North American Free Trade Agreement, with the two countries making progress on rules related to automobiles and other remaining issues during two days of meetings that ended on Friday in Washington.

A preliminary agreement between Mexico and the United States would go a long way toward accomplishing President Trump's goal of revising the quarter-century-old trade pact, which he has frequently criticized as the worst trade deal ever. But talks this week have excluded the pact's third member, Canada, leaving significant issues unresolved.

"The jury is still out on whether we'll get to a final agreement," said Michael C. Camuñez, the chief executive of Monarch Global Strategies and a former official at the Commerce Department. "But for the first time in negotiations, the U.S. seems to be negotiating from a genuine posture to get to a 'yes.' "

The Trump administration has described Canada as recalcitrant and would prefer to do a bilateral deal with Mexico first. But Mexican officials have insisted that Canada must still be part of the final agreement, which governs trade terms across the continent.

But an initial agreement between Mexico and the United States could help bring Canada back to the negotiating table to resolve the remaining differences, said Lori Wallach, the director of the Global Trade Watch at Public Citizen.

"I suspect their strategy to get Canada to re-engage is to settle their issues and then say to Canada, the water's nice, come on in," she said.

Speaking outside of the meetings on Thursday, Ildefonso Guajardo, the Mexican economy secretary, said that there had been "very good advancement" in the talks.

An Audi manufacturing production line in Mexico. One of the thorniest issues between the United States and Mexico has been the rules that govern whether automobiles qualify for zero tariffs under Nafta.

One of the thorniest issues between the United States and Mexico has been the rules that govern whether automobiles qualify for zero tariffs under Nafta. On this issue, Canada and the United States have much closer stances, said Antonio Ortiz-Mena, a senior vice president at the Albright Stonebridge Group.

"So if Mexico and the U.S. can agree on this, I think it should not be difficult for Canada to come on board," he said. Mexico and the United States do appear to be making progress on the issue, with Mexico expressing openness to a provision backed by the United States that would require a certain percentage of an automobile to be made with high-wage labor to qualify for Nafta's benefits.

Mexico and the United States are experiencing a new surge of motivation to close a deal after Andrés Manuel López Obrador was elected last month as Mexico's next president.

Negotiations over Nafta had reached a standstill this spring, with the three countries far apart on several key issues and Mexico taking a pause as it entered the final stages of its presidential campaign.

But now, with the election over, the departing administration of President Enrique Peña Nieto is eager to wrap up negotiations and secure a more business-friendly Nafta deal as part of its legacy before Mr. López Obrador moves into office. And Mr. López Obrador has expressed approval of the plan, viewing Nafta talks that would linger into his tenure as a potential distraction from his more domestic-focused policy agenda, analysts say.

But while Mexico may be more willing to compromise to reach a deal, the American posture toward the talks also may have started to shift.

Mr. Trump's tariff policies, and the retaliation they have prompted around the globe, have elicited criticism from Republican lawmakers and American industries, especially farmers, who say reduced access to foreign markets is crippling their businesses.

The complaints have become a looming issue in America's midterm elections, particularly as other countries like Japan and the European Union begin to strike their own trade deals that exclude the United States. The Trump administration also appears more eager to have the help of close allies like the European Union as it tries to force China to change its practices on trade. In late July, President Trump announced that the United States would work on resolving trade issues with the European Union, and that the two would work together to make changes that target China at the World Trade Organization.

But time is still running short for the current Mexican administration to reach a new Nafta agreement. Under current trade laws, the Trump administration must give Congress 90 days' notice between when it concludes negotiating a trade agreement and when it is signed. For Mr. Peña Nieto to sign the agreement before he leaves office on Nov. 30, the three countries must seal a final deal before Aug. 27, Ms. Wallach said.

Reaching an agreement could give the Trump administration ammunition to argue that it had fulfilled another major trade promise to revise Nafta. That could help populist Republicans, who echo Mr. Trump's trade views, win bragging rights ahead of the elections. But many details remain unsettled and it is unclear just how much of a revamp Canada will be willing to accept.

Mr. Trump began negotiations last August promising to swiftly overhaul Nafta, which he has long criticized for stealing American jobs. But his proposals for significantly changing the agreement, including forcing more automobile manufacturing into the United States and allowing members to more easily leave the pact, soon ran into opposition from the other governments as well as American businesses whose futures are tightly tied to Nafta.

Over the past year of negotiations, the Trump administration has repeatedly said it was racing to resolve Nafta talks before a deadline that it then failed to meet.

"In fairness we've seen this movie before," Mr. Camuñez said of the current, more promising state of play. He said it was hard to get too excited about the possibility of a final deal until Mr. Trump had demonstrated that he was firmly behind it.

"The administration giveth and the administration taketh away," he said. "The president himself is prone to change his mind on a whim."

# Trump Just Ripped Up Nafta. Here's What's in the New Deal.

BY JIM TANKERSLEY | OCT. 1, 2018

THERE'S A LOT to digest in the new trade agreement that the United States, Mexico and Canada finalized in deadline-beating fashion on Sunday, starting with a name change: If the new deal is adopted by all three countries, the North American Free Trade Agreement will give way to the United States-Mexico-Canada Agreement or U.S.M.C.A.

It's a cosmetic change for an otherwise consequential set of revisions.

"It's not Nafta redone, it's a brand-new deal," President Trump said at the White House on Monday.

Text of the pact, released late Sunday, includes major adjustments in several key areas of the countries' trading relationships. The agreement sets new rules for automobile production, meant to incentivize production of cars and trucks in countries that pay higher wages. It reduces barriers for American dairy farmers to sell cheese, milk and other products to Canada. It retains a tribunal for resolving trade disputes that the United States had sought to eliminate.

It guarantees Canadian and Mexican manufacturers expanded access to some large American markets, such as cars and light trucks, but leaves lingering questions about their ability to avoid tariffs on steel and aluminum exports to the United States.

Here are highlights from the text of the agreement, and from the 12 "side letters" the negotiating countries filed alongside it.

### An attempt to steer more car production to the United States

Nafta required automakers to produce 62.5 percent of a vehicle's content in North America to qualify for zero tariffs. The new agreement raises that threshold, over time, to 75 percent. That's meant to force automakers to source fewer parts for an "Assembled in Mexico" (or Canada) car from Germany, Japan, South Korea or China.

For the first time, the new agreement also mandates that an escalating percentage of parts for any tariff-free vehicle — topping out at 40 percent in 2023 — must come from a so-called "high wage" factory. The agreement says those factories must pay a minimum of $16 an hour in average salaries for production workers. That's about triple the average wage in a Mexican factory right now, and administration officials hope the provision will force automakers to shift suppliers from Mexico to Canada or the United States.

There are risks to that change. Automotive analysts have warned that the provision could have a damaging effect for Americans, by raising costs for American car buyers and incentivizing automakers to move production to low-cost countries outside the United States, such as China.

Conversely, the final provision, as written, could prove relatively ineffective at shifting production — because it is not indexed to inflation. An average wage of $16 an hour will be less constraining in 2023 dollars than it is today.

### Relief from future auto tariffs for Canada and Mexico

Mr. Trump has repeatedly threatened, over the last year, to impose tariffs on imported automobiles. In a news conference last week, he suggested that Canada would face such tariffs if it did not reach agreement with the United States on a new trade deal. Mr. Trump's administration has undertaken an investigation that could lead to auto tariffs, but it appears unlikely to finish up any time soon. The threat of auto tariffs has clouded trade talks with several countries, including Japan and South Korea, which import cars and car parts into America.

Canada and Mexico won't have to sweat it, though. The new agreement includes side letters that grant exemptions from any future American tariffs to 2.6 million imported passenger vehicles from each of those countries. That's slightly more vehicles than Mexico has exported to the United States over the last year, and nearly 1 million more than Canada has exported.

**Wins for American cheese (and wine)**

Perhaps the biggest sticking point in negotiations over the last month was the issue of Canada's protection of its dairy market, including limits on imported dairy products from the United States and government support that gives Canadian products an advantage on international markets against American ones.

"Dairy was a deal breaker," Mr. Trump said on Monday.

The new agreement gives the United States victories on both fronts. It gradually opens the Canadian market to more exported American dairy products, including "fluid milk, cream, butter, skim milk powder, cheese and other dairy products." Canada agreed to eliminate a program that helps Canadian sellers of certain milk products, at home and abroad.

It also creates a list of cheese names that Mexico and the United States agree can be marketed without restriction in their respective countries, and it forces grocery stores in British Columbia to stop their practice of selling British Columbia-only wines on certain shelves, and stock American wines alongside them.

**A win for Canada on dispute resolution**

Trade agreements typically come with enforcement mechanisms. As part of its renegotiation efforts, the United States sought to eliminate one of those mechanisms in Nafta: the so-called Chapter 19 provision, which gives the three countries a sort of neutral playing site — a panel with representatives from each country — to challenge each other's impositions of tariffs, and other actions.

Canada won the fight to keep that provision in the revised agreement. It did agree to eliminate another form of enforcement between the United States and Canada, which allows investors to sue for relief from foreign countries' actions. Consumer groups have long criticized that resolution mechanism, contending it allows large corporations too much power to challenge environmental and other regulations. The new deal leaves that mechanism in place for disputes between the United States and Mexico, but not for Canada.

**Goodies for unions, banks and pharmaceutical companies**

Among the small-but-significant items in the new agreement are a measure to push Mexico to make it easier for workers to form and join labor unions, steps to allow American financial services companies better access to Canadian and Mexican markets and a provision to extend the intellectual property protections of American pharmaceutical companies selling prescription drugs in Canada.

That last provision will grant longer protections to American biologic drugs, against biosimilar competitors, and it will probably raise the profits of those drugmakers when they sell in Canada.

# Glossary

**concession**  Something that is allowed or given up, usually during negotiations to end a disagreement.

**exemption**  The process of being free from an obligation or liability imposed on others.

**export**  To send goods or services to another country for sale.

**globalization**  The process where businesses or other organizations develop international influence or start operating on an international scale.

**import**  To bring goods or services into a country from abroad for sale.

**offshoring**  The practice of basing some of a company's services overseas, so as to take advantage of lower costs.

**pact**  A formal agreement between individuals or groups.

**protectionism**  The practice of protecting a country's domestic industries from foreign competition by taxing imports.

**quota**  A limited quantity of a particular product that under official controls can be produced, exported or imported.

**tariff**  A tax or duty to be paid on a particular class of imports or exports.

**trade barrier**  A government-induced restriction on international trade.

**trade deficit**  The amount by which the cost of a country's imports exceeds the value of its exports.

# Media Literacy Terms

"Media literacy" refers to the ability to access, understand, critically assess and create media. The following terms are important components of media literacy, and they will help you critically engage with the articles in this title.

**attribution**  The method by which a source is identified or by which facts and information are assigned to the person who provided them.

**balance**  Principle of journalism that both perspectives of an argument should be presented in a fair way.

**bias**  A disposition of prejudice in favor of a certain idea, person or perspective.

**credibility**  The quality of being trustworthy and believable, said of a journalistic source.

**editorial**  Article of opinion or interpretation.

**fake news**  A fictional or made-up story presented in the style of a legitimate news story, intended to deceive readers; also commonly used to criticize legitimate news because of its perspective or unfavorable coverage of a subject.

**impartiality**  Principle of journalism that a story should not reflect a journalist's bias and should contain balance.

**interview story**  Type of story in which the facts are gathered primarily by interviewing another person or persons.

**motive**  The reason behind something, such as the publication of a news story or a source's perspective on an issue.

**news story** An article or style of expository writing that reports news, generally in a straightforward fashion and without editorial comment.

**op-ed** An opinion piece that reflects a prominent individual's opinion on a topic of interest.

**paraphrase** The summary of an individual's words, with attribution, rather than a direct quotation of their exact words.

**plagiarism** An attempt to pass another person's work as one's own without attribution.

**quotation** The use of an individual's exact words indicated by the use of quotation marks and proper attribution.

**reliability** The quality of being dependable and accurate, said of a journalistic source.

**rhetorical device** Technique in writing intending to persuade the reader or communicate a message from a certain perspective.

**source** The origin of the information reported in journalism.

**style** A distinctive use of language in writing or speech; also a news or publishing organization's rules for consistent use of language with regards to spelling, punctuation, typography and capitalization, usually regimented by a house style guide.

**tone** A manner of expression in writing or speech.

# Media Literacy Questions

**1.** Compare the headlines of "Chance of Nafta Deal in 2018 Diminishes as Talks Drag Past Congressional Deadline" (on page 46) and "Trump Just Ripped Up Nafta. What's in the New Deal." (on page 207). Which is a more compelling headline, and why? How could the less compelling headline be changed to better draw the reader's interest?

**2.** What type of story is "Trump's Manchurian Trade Policy" (on page 51)? Can you identify another article in this collection that is the same type of story?

**3.** In " 'It's Factory North America,' but Trump Could Hobble It" (on page 75), Ana Swanson directly quotes two specific sources. What are the strengths of the use of a direct quote as opposed to a paraphrase? What are the weaknesses?

**4.** Does "Across Midwest, Farmers Warn of G.O.P. Losses Over Trump's Trade Policy" (on page 80) use multiple sources? What are the strengths of using multiple sources in a journalistic piece? What are the weaknesses of relying heavily on only one source or a few sources?

**5.** Identify the various sources cited in the article "A Storm of Reaction to Trump's Tariffs" (on page 131). How does The New York Times attribute information to each of these sources in the article? How effective are the attributions in helping the reader identify the sources?

**6.** "Anger Flares as G-7 Heads to Quebec" (on page 152) features a photograph. What does this photograph add to the article?

**7.** What is the intention of the article "What History Has to Say About the 'Winners' in Trade Wars" (on page 174)? How effectively does it achieve its intended purpose?

**8.** Identify each of the sources in "Trump Tariffs Threaten National Security" (on page 179) as a primary source or a secondary source. Evaluate the reliability and credibility of each source. How does your evaluation of each source change your perspective on this article?

**9.** The article "Chinese Tariffs Are Already Hitting Trump Voters" (on page 107) is an example of an editorial. Identify how The New York Times's editorial board's attitude and tone help convey their opinion on the topic.

**10.** Analyze the authors' reporting in "Trump's Steel Tariffs Raise Fears of a Damaging Trade War" (on page 169) and "United States and Mexico Are Nearing Nafta Compromise" (on page 203). Do you think one journalist is more balanced in their reporting than the other? If so, why do you think so?

**11.** This book features articles by both Ana Swanson and Jim Tankersley, as well as several articles they collaborated on together. Are there any noticeable differences in the tone and style of the articles they collaborated on compared to the articles they wrote separately?

# Citations

All citations in this list are formatted according to the
Modern Language Association's (MLA) style guide.

## BOOK CITATION

THE NEW YORK TIMES EDITORIAL STAFF. *Trade Wars: Tariffs in the 21st Century*.
New York: New York Times Educational Publishing, 2019.

## ONLINE ARTICLE CITATIONS

AUSTEN, IAN, AND DAN BILEFSKY. "Trump Says He Made Up Deficit Claim in
Talk with Trudeau, Baffling Canadians." *The New York Times*, 15 Mar. 2018,
https://www.nytimes.com/2018/03/15/world/canada/trump-trudeau-trade
.html.

BAKER, PETER. "Escalating Clash With Canada, Trump Is Isolated Before
North Korea Meeting." *The New York Times*, 10 June 2018, https://www
.nytimes.com/2018/06/10/us/politics/trump-trudeau-summit-g7-north
-korea.html.

BAKER, PETER, AND ANA SWANSON. "Trump Authorizes Tariffs, Defying Allies
at Home and Abroad." *The New York Times*, 8 Mar. 2018, https://www
.nytimes.com/2018/03/08/us/politics/trump-tariff-announcement.html.

BILEFSKY, DAN, AND CATHERINE PORTER. "Trump's 'Bully' Attack on Trudeau
Outrages Canadians." *The New York Times*, 10 June 2018, https://www
.nytimes.com/2018/06/10/world/canada/g-7-justin-trudeau-trump.html.

BOUDETTE, NEAL E. "G.M. Chief Cautions Trump Administration on Upending
Nafta." *The New York Times*, 16 Jan. 2018, https://www.nytimes.com/2018
/01/16/business/gm-nafta.html.

BRADSHER, KEITH, AND ALAN RAPPEPORT. "The Trade Issue That Most Divides
U.S. and China Isn't Tariffs." *The New York Times*, 26 Mar. 2018, https://
www.nytimes.com/2018/03/26/business/china-us-trade.html.

DAVIS, JULIE HIRSCHFELD, AND MARK LANDLER. "Trump Pitches 'America First'

Trade Policy at Asia-Pacific Gathering." *The New York Times*, 10 Nov. 2017, https://www.nytimes.com/2017/11/10/world/asia/trump-apec-asia-trade .html.

EWING, JACK. "U.S. Allies Jostle to Win Exemptions From Trump Tariffs." *The New York Times*, 9 Mar. 2018, https://www.nytimes.com/2018/03/09 /business/trump-tariffs-exemptions.html.

HILLMAN, JENNIFER A. "Trump Tariffs Threaten National Security." *The New York Times*, 1 June 2018, https://www.nytimes.com/2018/06/01/opinion /trump-national-security-tariffs.html.

KRUGMAN, PAUL. "Trump's Manchurian Trade Policy." *The New York Times*, 28 May 2018, https://www.nytimes.com/2018/05/28/opinion/trump -china-trade-policy.html.

LONDOÑO, ERNESTO, AND MOTOKO RICH. "U.S. Allies Sign Sweeping Trade Deal in Challenge to Trump." *The New York Times*, 8 Mar. 2018, https://www .nytimes.com/2018/03/08/world/asia/us-trump-tpp-signed.html.

MALKIN, ELISABETH, AND PAULINA VILLEGAS. "After Taunting Mexico, Trump Takes Action With Tariffs. But Do Mexicans Still Care?" *The New York Times*, 1 June 2018, https://www.nytimes.com/2018/06/01/world/americas /mexico-us-tariffs-steel-trump.html.

MARTIN, JONATHAN. "Across Midwest, Farmers Warn of G.O.P. Losses Over Trump's Trade Policy." *The New York Times*, 18 Apr. 2018, https://www .nytimes.com/2018/04/18/us/politics/trump-tariffs-china-soybeans -midterms.html.

THE NEW YORK TIMES. "Chinese Tariffs Are Already Hitting Trump Voters." *The New York Times*, 15 June 2018, https://www.nytimes.com/2018/06/15 /opinion/sunday/trump-china-tariffs-trade-farmers.html.

THE NEW YORK TIMES. "A Storm of Reaction to Trump's Tariffs." *The New York Times*, 8 Mar. 2018, https://www.nytimes.com/2018/03/08/business /economy/trump-tariff-reaction.html.

RAPPEPORT, ALAN. "Senators Ask White House Economists to Turn Over Tariff Findings." *The New York Times*, 14 June 2018, https://www.nytimes.com /2018/06/14/us/politics/senators-ask-white-house-economists-to-turn-over -tariff-findings.html.

RAPPEPORT, ALAN, AND ANA SWANSON. "Trump Expected to List China Tariffs, Potentially Reigniting Trade War." *The New York Times*, 14 June 2018, https://www.nytimes.com/2018/06/14/us/politics/trump-tariffs-china .html.

SCHREUER, MILAN. "E.U. Pledges to Fight Back on Trump Tariffs as Trade War Looms." *The New York Times*, 7 Mar. 2018, https://www.nytimes.com/2018/03/07/business/trump-tariffs-eu-trade.html.

SHEAR, MICHAEL D. "Anger Flares as G-7 Heads to Quebec." *The New York Times*, 7 June 2018, https://www.nytimes.com/2018/06/07/us/politics/trump-allies-g7-summit-meeting.html.

SHEAR, MICHAEL D., AND CATHERINE PORTER. "Trump Refuses to Sign G-7 Statement and Calls Trudeau 'Weak'." *The New York Times*, 9 June 2018, https://www.nytimes.com/2018/06/09/world/americas/donald-trump-g7-nafta.html.

STEVENSON ALEXANDRA, AND MOTOKO RICH. "Trans-Pacific Trade Partners Are Moving On, Without the U.S." *The New York Times*, 11 Nov. 2017, https://www.nytimes.com/2017/11/11/business/trump-tpp-trade.html.

STEWART, JAMES B. "What History Has to Say About the 'Winners' in Trade Wars." *The New York Times*, 8 Mar. 2018, https://www.nytimes.com/2018/03/08/business/tariff-trump-trade-wars.html.

SWANSON, ANA. " 'It's Factory North America,' but Trump Could Hobble It." *The New York Times*, 30 Mar. 2018, https://www.nytimes.com/2018/03/30/business/economy/trade-nafta-union-pacific.html.

SWANSON, ANA. "Trump Trade Measures Set Off a Global Legal Pushback." *The New York Times*, 9 Feb. 2018, https://www.nytimes.com/2018/02/09/us/politics/trump-trade.html.

SWANSON, ANA. "Trump Trade Sanctions Aimed at China Could Ensnare Canada." *The New York Times*, 25 Feb. 2018, https://www.nytimes.com/2018/02/25/business/trump-trade-sanctions-aimed-at-china-could-ensnare-canada.html.

SWANSON, ANA. "Trump's Tariffs Prompt Global Threats of Retaliation." *The New York Times*, 2 Mar. 2018, https://www.nytimes.com/2018/03/02/us/politics/trump-tariffs-steel-aluminum.html.

SWANSON, ANA. "Trump's Trade Policy Is Lifting Exports. Of Canadian Lobster." *The New York Times*, 12 Nov. 2017, https://www.nytimes.com/2017/11/12/business/trump-trade-lobster-canada.html.

SWANSON, ANA. "Trump Upends Global Trade Order Built by U.S." *The New York Times*, 10 June 2018, https://www.nytimes.com/2018/06/10/business/trump-trade-tariffs.html.

SWANSON, ANA. "United States and Mexico Are Nearing Nafta Compromise." *The New York Times*, 3 Aug. 2018, https://www.nytimes.com/2018/08/03

/us/politics/united-states-mexico-nafta.html.

SWANSON, ANA. "U.S. and China Expand Trade War as Beijing Matches Trump's Tariffs." *The New York Times*, 15 June 2018, https://www.nytimes .com/2018/06/15/us/politics/us-china-tariffs-trade.html.

SWANSON, ANA. "White House to Impose Metal Tariffs on E.U., Canada and Mexico." *The New York Times*, 31 May 2018, https://www.nytimes.com /2018/05/31/us/politics/trump-aluminum-steel-tariffs.html.

SWANSON, ANA. "Will 2018 Be the Year of Protectionism? Trump Alone Will Decide." *The New York Times*, 3 Jan. 2018, https://www.nytimes.com /2018/01/03/us/politics/2018-trump-protectionism-tariffs.html.

SWANSON, ANA, AND ELISABETH MALKIN. "Chance of Nafta Deal in 2018 Diminishes as Talks Drag Past Congressional Deadline." *The New York Times*, 17 May 2018, https://www.nytimes.com/2018/05/17/us/politics/nafta-deal -deadline-congress.html.

SWANSON, ANA, AND BRAD PLUMER. "Trump's Solar Tariffs Are Clouding the Industry's Future." *The New York Times*, 23 Jan. 2018, https://www .nytimes.com/2018/01/23/us/politics/trump-solar-tariffs.html.

SWANSON, ANA, AND JIM TANKERSLEY. "Mexico, Hitting Back, Imposes Tariffs on $3 Billion Worth of U.S. Goods." *The New York Times*, 5 June 2018, https://www.nytimes.com/2018/06/05/us/politics/trump-trade-canada -mexico-nafta.html.

SWANSON, ANA, AND JIM TANKERSLEY. "Potential Auto Tariffs Prompt Warnings From Industry and Allies." *The New York Times*, 24 May 2018, https://www .nytimes.com/2018/05/24/us/politics/trump-auto-tariffs-trade.html.

SWANSON, ANA, ET AL. "Trump's Tariffs Trigger Global Chain Reaction to Halt Imports." *The New York Times*, 27 Mar. 2018, https://www.nytimes.com /2018/03/27/business/trump-tariffs-imports.html.

TANKERSLEY, JIM. "Economists Say U.S. Tariffs Are Wrong Move on a Valid Issue." *The New York Times*, 11 Apr. 2018, https://www.nytimes.com/2018 /04/11/business/economy/trump-economists.html.

TANKERSLEY, JIM. "Trump Embraces a Trade War, Which Could Undermine Growth." *The New York Times*, 2 Mar. 2018, https://www.nytimes.com /2018/03/02/us/politics/trump-embraces-a-trade-war-which-could -undermine-growth.html.

TANKERSLEY, JIM. "Trump Just Ripped Up Nafta. Here's What's in the New Deal." *The New York Times*, 1 Oct. 2018, https://www.nytimes.com/2018 /10/01/business/trump-nafta-usmca-differences.html.

TANKERSLEY, JIM. "Trump's Steel Tariffs Raise Fears of a Damaging Trade War." *The New York Times*, 2 Mar. 2018, https://www.nytimes.com/2018/03/02/business/trump-tariffs-trade-war.html.

TANKERSLEY, JIM, AND NATALIE KITROEFF. "U.S. Exempts Some Allies From Tariffs, but May Opt for Quotas." *The New York Times*, 22 Mar. 2018, https://www.nytimes.com/2018/03/22/business/us-eu-tariffs-steel-aluminum.html.

TANKERSLEY, JIM, AND ANA SWANSON. "Trump's Trade Moves Put U.S. Carmakers in a Jam at Home and Abroad." *The New York Times*, 10 May 2018, https://www.nytimes.com/2018/05/10/us/politics/trump-auto-industry-trade.html.

# Index

$39.95

**LONGWOOD PUBLIC LIBRARY**
800 Middle Country Road
Middle Island, NY 11953
(631) 924-6400
longwoodlibrary.org

**LIBRARY HOURS**

| | |
|---|---|
| Monday-Friday | 9:30 a.m. - 9:00 p.m. |
| Saturday | 9:30 a.m. - 5:00 p.m. |
| Sunday (Sept-June) | 1:00 p.m. - 5:00 p.m. |